NOT THERE YET

NOT THERE YET

Living through Egypt, Love,
and Uncertainty – A Memoir

Catherine Manfre

NEW DEGREE PRESS

NOT THERE YET

Living through Egypt, Love, and Uncertainty – A Memoir

ISBN

979-8-88504-544-5   *Paperback*

979-8-88504-870-5   *Kindle Ebook*

979-8-88504-660-2   *Digital Ebook*

This book is dedicated to my parents who always supported and loved me, my brothers who inspired me to become a role model, my incredible husband who supports every new or ambitious goal I set for myself — no matter how big, and my precious daughter who motivates me every day to work to create a better world she can inherit.

CONTENTS

———

"I believe in life and in people. I feel obliged to advocate their highest ideals as long as I believe them to be true."

— NAGUIB MAHFOUZ, SUGAR STREET

Some names in this book are real and others
have been given pseudonyms, but all are
based on real people and conversations.

In many cases I refer to conversations
with "Egyptian friends" to protect those
who still live in Egypt, where the situation
surrounding freedom of speech remains fluid.

The events in this book rely on my
recollections and research.

AUTHOR'S NOTE

———

January 6th, 2021. I was celebrating the milestone of keeping my daughter alive for about as long as I grew her inside of me (a milestone, I think, should be added to the list of celebratory milestones). That time spent keeping her safe during a global pandemic was punctuated with incredible uncertainty. I do not know what it is like to become or be a parent otherwise, but constantly weighing the risks associated with being near other humans felt absolutely exhausting. As if scary parenting articles were not enough.

The days blended together in a soup of memories.

We found refuge around the Washington, DC, area where we could enjoy being around people from a distance. One of those places included the National Mall, the stretch of grass between the Capitol, the Washington Monument, and the Lincoln Memorial. The vast expanse allowed us to people watch from far away and enjoy the outside air separately but together. Only a fifteen-minute drive from our townhouse in Northeast Washington, DC, we were frequent visitors; the National Mall was our backyard and the Capitol our sentinel watching over us, protecting us.

But then my phone started buzzing with news alerts about protests at the Capitol. Not unusual. The buzzing continued.

The word protest turned into "storm," "breach." Finally, I turned the news on, my 9-month-old daughter sitting on my lap. The news felt so urgent, important, and local I kept the TV on despite my new parenting obsession with keeping her away from screens.

Meanwhile, my close friend who lives blocks from the Capitol texted to see if her, her husband, and her two young kids could possibly stay with us that evening. Of course, was my answer, putting aside fears of COVID exposure risk after close to a year lockdown.

I sat on the edge of my seat, in mostly disbelief at the images on my screen. I say mostly because there were obvious breadcrumbs leading to the events of those days, clues about our arrival at what seemed like a full-blown midlife crisis about the identity of our country.

It felt obvious to me we had arrived at an inflection point, a crossroads. This was not my first time living in a country going through an identity crisis. I have lived through moments when a country needs to decide which street to cross or which road to take.

I lived in a different country on a different date in January ten years earlier. On January 25, 2011, the Egyptian revolution, packaged as part of the "Arab Spring," began. I had been living and working in Cairo, Egypt for over two years when Egyptians took to the streets. On that day I, like so many others, thought Egyptian security forces would quickly and firmly crack down and prevent any serious dissent. I assumed the protests would be small and over swiftly despite the buzz in the country about President Hosni Mubarak's staying power.

That, of course, did not happen.

When I returned to live in the US a year and a half after Mubarak resigned, I frequently got asked about what it was like "living through a revolution." Often, I made jokes to deflect from the longer, more complicated answer. Sometimes, I'd bullet point the three main moods I observed during that time: hope, fear, uncertainty. But the longer answer of what leads a group of citizens to take to the streets and what compels ordinary citizens to lay down their lives and livelihoods is much more complicated. It involves the deterioration of trust in government, absence of support services, limited economic opportunity, systemic economic and social inequality, and fear for the future. Usually, a powerful propaganda machine helps to push people to stay home or not, depending on the objectives of the day. And Egypt had many of these problems too.

I couldn't immediately figure out why January 6th triggered memories of January 25th. They felt totally different in objective and practically mirror images — one group tearing down democracy and the other demanding it.

Why did memories of my time leading up to, during, and in the post-revolution aftermath in Egypt flood my thoughts? Why, in the months after January 6th, could I not stop thinking about the military tanks that became commonplace in post-Mubarak Egypt? Why did memories of sporadic protests, violence, and fear come rushing back to me? What caused me to remember the bravery of Egyptian protesters and the hope that filled the space between fear and uncertainty after Mubarak resigned? What made me so angry when my fellow Americans seemed to dismiss January 6th or not remember it at all? Why was January 6th still an event that feels so shocking and urgent for us to address?

Why did I feel compelled to tell my story?

When I first stepped foot in Egypt, I was a college student, still a teenager. I moved full time to Egypt right after graduation and had never lived an adult life in America. I had never filed taxes or signed a lease or had my own health insurance.

I arrived in Egypt with two filled-to-the-brim suitcases and an idealistic image of my own country, America, clearly etched in my head. I carried the image of what it meant to be American and live in a "free" country where if you worked hard enough and wanted something badly enough, then anything was possible. I was told my whole life that I could be anyone and do anything. I believed it. I believed our country was fair, just, and equal. I had learned our history but believed, for the most part, it was exactly that despite glimpses of inequity and injustice growing up.

When I got to Egypt I was confronted with a very different world. It often felt like walking through libraries of history just walking down one street in Cairo. And I could never get over the sight of the Pyramids of Giza no matter how many times I drove past or saw them from the plane window upon the final descent into Cairo International Airport. Egyptian culture is filled with humor and warmth and friendliness and religion and family and community. But living in Egypt could also feel like living in a dodgeball game — I never knew what would be flying at me and I needed to be constantly prepared.

Many know Egypt from her ancient treasures and lengthy past. The Egypt I grew to know and love (most days) very much lives in the present, with current beauty, personality quirks, wit, and a live set of challenges. She is both compassionate and loving while also an experiential and sometimes direct teacher. She became my home and gave me my greatest joy.

At first, I often and annoyingly compared Egypt to America. I would say, "Well, in the US we wouldn't do this," or "In the US we would do this better," or "in the US this would never happen." My expat friends and I did this to cope with the wildly different culture and country we were trying to make home as much as we genuinely believed the comparisons. The comparisons were sometimes trivial, like Egyptians' refusal to form lines, but were sometimes big, like the inability to openly criticize the Egyptian government.

At some point, I stopped (for the most part) making those comparisons to the great relief of my Egyptian friends and began to experience and appreciate Egypt and Egyptian culture. At some point, I met the love of my life. This is also a love story.

I do not seek to make comparisons in my story, but rather to reflect and learn.

I learned what it felt like to live under an authoritarian ruler with absolute political power and control over a country. I saw what happened without adequate investment in government and civil society institutions. A measure of government success is melting into the fabric of society itself, working so well an average citizen does not even realize government is happening. But what happens when you call the equivalent of 911 and no one answers or comes at all?

I also felt the cynicism of my Egyptian friends that nothing would ever change. I witnessed the courage of everyday Egyptians who took to the streets in 2011 to demand change. I felt the hope after they forced Mubarak's resignation. I saw the devastation at the close call of achieving a freer society with greater opportunities.

I saw Egypt at a crossroads.

Similarly, I worry very much about current day America. In the years since returning to America, I was reeducated about our country's own deficiencies — freedom and equality did not touch every American and those truths we hold self-evident are not quite so evident or accessible. I realized we share many of the same struggles as Egypt — the struggle for power, the balance of opportunity, women's rights and equity, the ability to live a free and hopeful life. Many of the challenges of a society do not change because of its placement on a map. Our common challenges and humanity can help build bridges.

Living in Egypt, I realized the numerous, seemingly mundane activities I took for granted: to travel easily to many countries around the world, to participate in elections without pre-determined outcomes, to consume news and media free from government oversight and intervention, and to access grocery stores with 20,000 plus items. My time in Egypt made me realize what it meant to have privilege and not even know it.

In the US, I saw the warning signs of pre-revolution Egypt — news turning toward propaganda, misinformation being believed as truth, limitations on the ability to vote or peacefully protest. Surely this is not our path, I thought, that's not where we are going.

However, when I watched the events of January 6th unfolding on my screen, I began to wonder if perhaps I was wrong.

We are at another inflection point in our history. We need to decide what destination we want to reach so we can choose which road to go down. One road leads to fewer freedoms to participate, fewer chances to disagree, fewer opportunities to succeed. The other road looks more like my teenage image of America that traveled with me on my first flight to Egypt — the image that was part of my baggage. Following this path leads to becoming more inclusive to all kinds of diversity and creating equitable ways of attaining economic security and success. This destination holds the promise of something better — equitable opportunity, freedom, justice, progress, and peace. It is the same path Egyptians, and so many other people around the world, want.

We can get there, but we're not there yet.

My biggest takeaway is the types of systemic change needed to meet the demands of a revolution or to create greater equity in society are *really* hard. And they certainly cannot happen if people do not know how to talk to each other — even if only to disagree.

I hope my story provides a glimpse of what can happen when a country's population has limited hope for individual economic stability and limited opportunity for political or societal participation. Also, I hope my story can serve as a mirror to reflect what feels familiar in an uncomfortable way. Common ground can create dialogue, but it can also serve as a trail marker of where we want to be.

Let me show you one path.

CHAPTER 1:

A BIG EVENT

September 11, 2001.

I walked down the crowded hallway in the main freshman building of my high school located in a small county in Northeast Florida. Olive green lockers stood ready for their owners to bang them open and closed, to grab books for the next class, or to operate as meeting posts. Classroom doors on the other side of the hallway stood open, teachers watched to make sure the newly-minted high schoolers behaved as they acclimated to newfound high school freedoms.

The barren painted cinderblock was punctuated with carefully curated "back to school" posters and reminders hung by teachers eager to instill class unity and school spirit. Like guests in someone's home, even the pranksters had not yet felt enough ownership over their surroundings to poke fun at these attempts at housewarming. Green and white, our school colors, accented the otherwise colorless hallways.

Not yet instinctually finding the bathrooms or skipping the stalls with a broken lock, I still felt like our sprawling Florida campus felt impossibly large. A rule follower, I felt petrified of arriving to class late. I practically ran from class to class since I frequently landed in the wrong building and then needed to sprint in the other direction to get to class; the seven minutes allotted between most classes never felt like enough time. The upperclassmen all seemed impossibly older, more mature, cooler, and totally sure of the world. I could barely remember what textbook I needed for the next class because, of course, I had insisted on taking the most rigorous course load possible; I was one of those little girls who felt seen for the first time in the character Hermione Granger from the *Harry Potter* series. My books felt as heavy as my near constant stress level from surviving my first few weeks of high school

Blessedly, my high school had an extended gap between the first and second period of the day called "Bulldog Break," which gave many students a chance to grab something to eat or get a burst of energy from talking to friends before settling in for the morning stretch of classes until lunch. Most of us had not discovered the power of a cup of coffee, so we relied on teenage angst to wake us up and get through the day.

Barely fully awake, despite being one full class into the day, I stood at my locker doing a quick check in the mirror that was carefully attached to my locker door, while talking to a friend. Just then, breaking through the normal high school white noise, a classmate known for playing pranks came running down the hall half-yelling and half-laughing.

"A plane flew into the World Trade Center!" he yelled.

He had a huge smile on his face, which made it unclear if he was trying to push the hallway full of already anxious, nervous freshmen over the edge or if he simply found the news absurd. From his tone, it did not strike me to be nervous or afraid at this news; I wasn't immediately sure I even believed him.

This was the era of flip phones with little more than the phone game "Snake" as entertainment. No one could log into social media or check a news app; our only way to socially discuss media was turning to the person next to us, our only source of speculation.

"Wait, is the World Trade Center the same thing as the Twin Towers? Or is that something different?"

"Is that in New York?"

"Aren't those the tallest buildings in the country? How could someone miss them?"

"The pilot must be pretty dumb to run into a skyscraper."

But many, even most, of my peers quickly turned back to their conversations, treating the disruption like a brief commercial break in their sitcom of high school gossip and drama. None of us considered that someone flew a plane into a building on purpose. The only thing I felt attacked by were homework assignments and the emerging popular kids.

So, we all went to our next class, worried about pop quizzes and half completed homework assignments, not knowing our entire lives were about to change.

We felt safe and protected in our high school bubble, insulated from world events.

Our small Flagler County rarely made news.

Flagler County was created in 1917 when land was carved off from two neighboring counties as a tribute to Henry Flagler who built the Florida East Coast Railway (Kent, 2020). It is located two hours south of the Georgia border. St. Augustine, the oldest city in the country, borders Flagler to the north, Daytona —with its NASCAR races, spring break attraction, and bike week— to the south, and the ocean to the east. For most, Flagler is a place between places: a quick bathroom break while driving down I-95 or a surprising stretch of coastal highway with unobstructed views of the ocean.

My family and I moved to Flagler from Long Island, NY, two years earlier, making me endure a change of schools in the middle of middle school. The city we moved to, Palm Coast, FL, became an incorporated city the year we moved in 1999. Like many, my parents came to pursue new opportunities and escape New York winters. My younger brothers and I were excited to live in a constant vacation setting and play year-round sports, forgetting at the ages of twelve, ten, and two that the rhythms of normal life still apply.

Despite the newness of Palm Coast's history, it already had a few quirks. Palm Coast was developed by a large real estate development company, so instead of streets with names honoring historic figures or places, they divided the city into lettered "sections" where all the streets started with the same letter. When we first moved to Palm Coast we lived in the "W" section on a street called Walnut. Walnut connected to Walker, connected to Wynnfield, with other connecting streets named Waters, Williams, Warner, Wilden, Warner, Warren, Winterling, and Wasserman.

Many of these lettered sections were littered with houses with long stretches of undeveloped land between them, waiting for an owner to purchase the land and build a stucco house. Many people, like my family, did exactly that.

Our biggest claim to fame was not the willowing, wild, weird (okay, I'll stop) naming convention of our streets, but that Flagler County became one of the fastest growing counties in the country from 2000 to 2005 (Associated Press, 2006). When we moved to Flagler in 1999, the population was only about 50,000 people. That number doubled to 100,000 by 2010 (U.S. Census Bureau, 2022). Many families, like mine, came from the Northeast, creating a melting pot of cultures and backgrounds in our tiny, mainly agrarian county.

Flagler, like so much of Florida, is a place where most people are from somewhere else.

However, there were some families who had been long-time Flagler County residents, who traced their heritage back several or more generations. Many of those families lived on the West side of the county, an area primarily dedicated to farming.

Because of this population explosion, my high school was bursting at the seams. The rapid expansion in the population seemed to have left school planners flat-footed, meaning Flagler Palm Coast High School was the only high school in the county. Despite new buildings to accommodate, some of my classes were in "portables" — temporary structures outside the main building that were either way too hot or way too cold and, in those early days of high school, impossible to find.

Flagler Palm Coast High School hadn't always been the only high school in the county. From the 1949 to 1967 school year, two high schools existed in Flagler: Bunnell High School for white students and George Washington Carver High School for black students. In 1967, the county began allowing voluntary integration and the class of 1968's Bunnell High School yearbook depicts a multi-racial class for the first time.

The 1968 Bunnell High School yearbook includes only 14 graduating seniors and a detailed description of the graduating classes' progression from kindergarten onwards; it described which students joined the school and when, along with commentary on major milestones the class experienced together, from winning the Homecoming parade float contest to senior exams. However, the newly integrated Black students got only this mention: "We gained six new students our senior year."

In his note to the graduating class Principal Kenneth Harding wrote this about the integration of the two high schools: "The school year 1967-68 has been a challenging one for all of us. Since there is so much change in our society these days, we must be prepared to accept these changes and strive for even higher goals. This will especially affect the seniors, who will be taking their places in our adult society within a few days."

Two years later, in 1970, the U.S. Department of Justice mandated integration for Flagler County. That summer Bunnell High School erupted in flames and many believed the fire was set intentionally, although no one were ever charged (Hoye, 2013). Flagler County Public Schools appealed the decision. The United States Court of Appeals, Fifth Circuit in *U.S. vs. Flagler County School District* ruled against the district in March of 1972 and mandated integration.

Thirty years later, Confederate flag paraphernalia was a common sight in my high school.

Yet I could not wear shorts in the Florida summer heat because of our school dress code. *Right.*

I learned about the numerous flags of the Confederacy from the back of a classmate's T-shirt I had to stare at while sitting in a U.S. history class. He had a collection of T-shirts with Confederate flags, seemingly one for each day of the month. Not that he was alone. Cars in the school parking lot proudly displayed bumper stickers proclaiming, "The South Will Rise Again." To this day a large Confederate flag flies high, intentionally in full sight of I-95 near an exit close to my hometown.

Our pristine coastline and palm trees could make these realities easy to miss.

Otherwise, Flagler Palm Coast High School felt like something out of an angsty high school drama with cliques of students who quickly sorted themselves by stereotype. There were the athletes, the honors students, the thespians, and the surfer kids. There were also the kids who lived on the west side of the county who sometimes threw parties in the blueberry fields on the weekends. Many from that part of town participated in Cracker Day, the annual rodeo and county fair that featured events like barrel racing and prizes for the largest steer or pig. "Cracker" was also the nickname given to early cowboys and the name of a small horse used to herd cattle (Cody, 2011)

Cutting across many of those groups, were the many, many kids whose families had moved from out of state or "up north," like mine.

For some students in my high school, New York City and the World Trade Center felt like another world — a place outside our blinders of high school and difficult to imagine given higher priorities like exams and love interests. But for others, like me, New York still felt closer to home than Flagler County.

Once the Morse-code-like bell rang, signaling we had a minute to get to class before becoming "late," students ran or meandered to the next class. I shuffled along with the herd of students.

I sat down in my usual seat; my teacher clearly agitated.

"Class, given the evolving events, I'm going to turn on the news instead of our usual lesson and we can discuss what is happening," she said.

My teacher had been teaching for decades and had a reputation for not deviating from her planned agenda. When she announced our lesson would be watching and discussing the news, I felt concerned for the first time that morning.

We sat there watching the first tower burn, exchanging naïve and limited commentary, while the on-air reporters tried to make sense of what was happening. We just sat and sat and sat, watching.

We watched as the second plane came onto the screen and hit the second tower. We watched as we heard the news of the plane flying into the Pentagon. We watched as the fourth plane, destined for the Capitol, crashed in Pennsylvania.

I sat there not knowing what feelings I should have. It felt like a movie. It couldn't be real, right?

Shortly after, our school went into lockdown, which meant no one could leave the classroom unless we had to go to the bathroom.

We watched as news reporters tried and struggled to react in real time. They were using words that few of us really had heard before like "terrorist." I did not understand what they meant. It was difficult enough to try and process that these planes were intentionally flying into buildings. All planes in the country were grounded. Kids' parents started arriving at the school to pick them up.

I sat with my class for what felt like hours. Few if any of us had cell phones nor did we have laptops or iPads, so we were connected to the rest of the world only through the TV. I had no way of contacting my parents. I only had my teacher and fellow classmates to try and process the new information catapulting off the screen. The concerns I had only hours earlier seemed remote and silly.

Suddenly, living in a small town in Florida seemed like the safest place to live despite my routine complaints to my parents since moving from New York to Florida.

Eventually, sometime in the early afternoon, my mom came and picked me up. My mom typically wears her emotions like a piece of clothing. But that day, I had no idea what she was thinking or feeling. I don't even recall us talking as she picked me up. It was like the fear of the day had wiped out her ability to emote.

My dad was the county sheriff at the time. We did not see him very frequently in the weeks that followed as he was on numerous calls and meetings to ensure the safety of the county residents and the safety of the people of Florida. In the month that followed, my vocabulary drastically expanded to include words I had, at best, only a vague awareness of like, Islam, Saudi Arabia, Afghanistan, terrorism.

After 9/11, some upperclassmen began joining the military; military recruiters became a constant presence in our cafeteria. Others had an almost immediate anger towards Muslims and people from Muslim countries. I didn't know the word then, but it was my first taste of xenophobia.

Many, if not most, students mainly seemed glad to have missed tests or homework assignments.

My friends and I learned as much as we could. We frequently debated the events of the day, why it happened, and its impact. Some teachers entertained our distraction with world events in place of some our typical lessons, while others seemed keen to shut out world events, to create a seemingly safe space devoid of outside influence.

For the remainder of my freshman year, I was getting a parallel education — my school education and world education. My fourteen-year-old self went on this quest to make sense of what happened, to find an explanation, and to rationalize how the world could create such anger and hatred to make people want to kill a large group of people.

It was living in a history textbook or maybe an action movie. I couldn't decide which.

A year later, I sat in an Advanced Placement U. S. History class, which was a small class of around ten people. We frequently got new students throughout the year and it was not surprising when a school administrator walked in partially through the year and ushered in a new student.

"Class, we have a new student today," my teacher said. "Her name is Arfa."

CHAPTER 2:

A NEW FRIEND

"Arfa just moved here with her family. Class, can you say hello to Arfa?"

"Hi Arfa," we all said, not quite in unison. In walked a girl who looked different than almost everyone in my high school. Her family, originally from Pakistan, had just moved from Southern Maryland to Flagler County. According to U.S. Census Bureau data in 2000, Flagler County was about 84% white, 10% black, and 5% Hispanic or Latino; there was almost no one from her background in the county much less in our high school.

Arfa did not say much in class at first and many students did not know how to begin a conversation with her. One day, I found myself paired with her during a class discussion exercise. We quickly veered off the discussion questions as I was curious to get to know her.

"So where did you move from?" I asked.

"A small town in Southern Maryland. I moved with my two brothers and twin sister," she said.

"You have a twin sister? What classes is she taking?" I asked, assuming she went to our school as well.

"She is deaf actually. We moved here so she could attend a better high school in St. Augustine."

"Oh wow, that must be tough. Do you know sign language?"

"Yes, our whole family learned it when we were young," she replied.

Our teacher began walking in our direction, so I quickly switched topics.

"Yes Arfa, that's such a great point about the main root causes of the American Civil War," I said.

My teacher glared at us, knowing we had not been discussing anything close to American history moments before. Arfa giggled.

As soon as my teacher was out of range though we continued our discussion. I told her about my own move several years before to Palm Coast and my experience as the new kid in middle school moving from New York. She told me about her experience so far in our high school, the difficulty of making friends as the new kid in class. We quickly realized we lived in the same neighborhood, less than a mile apart. Her mom had been driving her to school, so she hadn't ridden my bus.

We continued the conversation into the hallway: we swapped stories about being new kids in Palm Coast, poked fun at the numerous absurdities of the city, and commiserated about the lack of a decent movie theater and the need to drive at least thirty minutes to get to a semi-fashionable clothing store. We both wanted to have careers in public service or non-profits, something that would allow us to change the world. Both of us were rule followers but we were so distracted by our conversation we were practically late for our next class. We met up after school and continued our montage of teenage hopes and dreams and shared experiences. Before we realized it, we were practically inseparable.

Once I got my driver's license, I drove us to school every morning, and we constantly battled over which radio station or CD to play in the car.

"Arfa, come on, let's listen to this new CD I burned this weekend," I said.

"If I have to listen to Dashboard Confessional or Taking Back Sunday one more time, I think I might walk to school," she replied. "I just got a CD by this new rapper named Kanye West, could we listen to that instead? It's called 'College Dropout' and it's amazing. Genius even."

"Ugh, fine. You win."

A week later, Arfa could rap along to practically every song. She spent many hours trying to convince me of the lyrical genius of various hip-hop artists by dissecting the lyrics line by line. I still prefer angsty emo music.

Other than music, we had a lot in common. We both were top of our classes (Arfa was a grade above me), we both had big ambitions for our future, and we both had a shared, bedrock belief that we wanted to change the world — and that the world would let us. And obviously, we both loved talking about potential love interests.

We took an Advanced Placement Biology class together, one of the first times our school offered the course. Our teacher had never taught the class before and practically learned the material alongside us. I quickly decided I had a better chance of eventually passing the exam at the end of the year by doing a self-study of the material, while only half paying attention in class and spending time in the evening studying the textbook alone. Arfa, however, always trying to do the right thing, attempted to pay attention as my teacher explained cellular enzyme structure and photosynthesis. Meanwhile, I sat next to her on a lab stool trying to distract her from the lesson.

To do this, I would draw her and her crush of the week's name over and over again painfully in her line of sight. She would glare at me and roll her eyes or pretend to take notes so she could hide a smile. While she tried to studiously count the traits of our fruit fly progeny to understand dominant and recessive genes, I would crack juvenile jokes to throw off her careful counting.

Looking back, I would like to sincerely apologize to my poor teacher who patiently put up with our (mostly my) antics in that class. Teaching biology to a class of teenagers sounds now like a punishment.

I played for our high school lacrosse team and encouraged Arfa to try out. We had late fall conditioning sessions before tryouts in the winter so I told her she could come see if she liked it before committing.

"I definitely want to, but I'm not sure I can until after Ramadan ends," she said.

"What's Ramadan?" Why can't you come out during Ramadan?" I asked.

"Ramadan is the holy month in Islam. I'll be fasting, so it will be almost impossible to be doing a lot of exercise, especially late in the day," she said.

"What do you mean you'll be fasting?"

"During Ramadan we fast from sunrise to sundown. So, if conditioning is after school, I won't have eaten or had anything to drink all day," she said.

"You don't eat or drink anything all day? And you do that for an entire month?" I asked incredulously. "Why would you do that?"

Arfa, very patiently, went on to explain the purpose of Ramadan in Islam and why many Muslims spend an entire month fasting. She explained how they had a big meal once the sun went down called *iftar* which means "break a fast" and how they often spent many evenings with friends or going to the mosque. This opened a floodgate of questions from me about Islam.

We began meeting up at the basketball court in our neighborhood almost exactly equidistant between our houses. Neither of us were very good (although Arfa disputes this assessment of her skills), so often we resorted to games like "Horse" instead of playing an actual game. Most of our time though was spent sitting on the court and talking.

She opened up to me about how students at her last school frequently bullied her because of her Pakistani heritage, comments which grew worse after 9/11. She also told me how lonely it felt being different and how she often wished she had the courage to stand up to people who made nasty comments. She described how terrified she sometimes felt going to school right after 9/11, never knowing when the next taunt or cruel comment would come. I promised her that I would be with her if anything like that happened again.

Those basketball court conversations became the foundation of our lifelong friendship.

The first time I went to her house, something that became practically a ritual under the auspices of "studying," I noticed several framed pictures with an unreadable script.

"What's that on your wall?" I asked.

"Those are verses, or *suras*, of the Qur'an," she said.

"What's the Qur'an?"

"The Qur'an is the holy book in Islam, it's like the Bible but for Muslims," she said.

I got the sense she had been asked these basic Islam 101 questions before. She again patiently explained how Muslims believed the Qur'an had been revealed to the Prophet

Muhammed directly from God and how most Muslims follow any reference to him with "peace be upon him." From my mountain of follow-up questions, I learned the Qur'an is written in Arabic and that many Muslims pray five times a day, make sure a Qur'an never touches the ground, and pray in the direction of Mecca in current day Saudi Arabia. Even non-Arabic speaking Muslims, like Arfa's family, typically learn the Qur'an in its original Arabic.

I also got a literal taste of her heritage.

Not long after I became a regular visitor at her house, her mother asked me to stay for dinner so I could taste authentic Pakistani food.

"Catherine, do you normally eat spicy foods?" her mother asked, clearly having cooked for someone not accustomed to Pakistani food before.

"Umm, not really," I said.

"No problem, I'll make sure yours is very mild," she said.

We sat down at the table to eat, and Arfa's parents gave me an in-depth explanation of each dish: chicken tikka, vegetable pakora, naan, sweet and coriander chutney. The rice was the only familiar dish on the table. But I dug into the food, nonetheless.

My face almost instantly turned bright red, and I drank almost the entire glass of water next to my plate. Arfa started laughing.

"If that's very mild, I can't imagine what mild or moderate is like," I said. "But it's very tasty, thank you so much for cooking it," I continued trying my best not to be rude.

"It's okay Cat, you're not the first person we have had over who can't handle a little spice," she said with a grin, taking the opportunity to have a little fun at my expense.

"Arfa, why don't you get Catherine some yogurt to go with her food?" her mom interjected.

I needed the entire container of yogurt.

Arfa and her family were the first Muslims I remember knowing. I struggled to understand how Islam could be so generous and beautiful — her family was the living embodiment of warmth and generosity— and, on the other hand, be so perverted by the terrorists on 9/11. My conclusion was that terrorists and terrorism have nothing to do with a particular religion.

Unfortunately, not everyone agreed.

Arfa had told me many stories about comments people had made to her or her family about her background and assumptions people made about what her family must believe. Hearing second hand the prejudice she faced rocked my belief in the goodness of people and the justice I thought existed in the world. But one day, I got to see it too.

One normal day, we walked into school together, talking about nothing important but still taking ourselves very seriously. Our school population had ballooned to over 2,000, which made it difficult for anyone to know everyone. Despite the size, Arfa stuck out because there were so few people like her.

We walked into the crowded front lobby, and one of the two women working the front desk called out across the crowd of students.

"Hey, Osama's niece, you have a message from the front office."

I could feel Arfa immediately tense up. Neither of us were confused about the recipient of the woman's comment, despite the crowd of students in the lobby area. From all our talks I knew this was not Arfa's first time hearing a derogatory comment. I also knew that she typically preferred to ignore and say nothing to avoid further confrontation. She knew that I disagreed with that plan of inaction.

We walked over to the woman; Arfa looked like she saw a ghost, while I glared daggers at the woman. Arfa got her message while I seethed.

In my head, I yelled at the woman for her hatred, her ignorance, and her callousness.

"How can you work in a school and promote such intolerance? Don't you see that you're being rude and insensitive! How could you make the kindest person in the world feel so awful?" I yelled, internally. I kept all it all in my head because I loved Arfa. I knew how much she did not want me to say anything, and I knew all she wanted to do was run away from the situation and get on with her day.

As soon as we were out of earshot, all my opinions came pouring out of me about how totally wrong, inappropriate, racist, bigoted, and terrible the woman. My protectiveness over Arfa and sense of injustice blinded me to how Arfa's own feelings and what she needed from me in that moment.

I realized decades later that perhaps a more understanding, empathetic response would have been to ask Arfa how she was feeling and not comment on the cosmic injustice of the moment.

In the days that followed, we discussed the incident frequently. Arfa felt incredibly embarrassed and mortified. High school is tough enough without a school employee pointing out a difference you are already acutely aware of, particularly when that difference is on the lips of most TV news talking heads and our peers.

A couple weeks later, the woman said it again. Now it was a trend, not a one-off incident.

Arfa did not want to do or say anything. She felt like nothing would come of saying anything and it might even make things worse. But I, remembering my promise to her on the basketball court and filled with teenage rage at the injustice, marched into the principal's office during lunchtime without telling Arfa and told him what had happened. I knew my friend was in pain, and I knew what this school employee said was wrong. Those two facts carried my feet into the principal's office without me telling them to go. Both of us were called to the principal's office the next day. He asked Arfa what happened, and she told him what the woman had said. I tried to keep my mouth shut so she could tell her story.

He listened to us and said the right things. But I didn't get the sense he truly understood how deeply the comment cut. He committed to speaking to the woman, and, while that didn't seem like enough justice to me, it was clear the conversation was over. We had said our peace and now the wheels of justice needed to turn.

Later that week, the woman came up to Arfa and said, "Hey, Osama's niece, I didn't mean that to be offensive. I thought you knew it was a joke."

I understand the incredible privilege at this being the first bigoted comment I remember hearing. I also understand the privilege of it not being directed at me but at my best friend. However, my trust in justice chipped away.

I learned something Arfa clearly already knew — justice does not simply happen by pointing out injustice.

In my head, the sequence of events should have been the following: see something, say something, learn something, do something differently. That last part, I came to learn from years of experience, often does not happen. More often, people do the same thing they have been doing over and over and over again. That's what makes justice, progress, and change so difficult.

I also learned some people are intentional their bigotry. Many of us are a product of our upbringing and need to unlearn our ignorance and fear of those that are different. I also know many people are comfortable in their mistrust and intentionally hurt those around them for the "crime" of being different.

Learning both of those lessons simultaneously felt impossible and adult.

I was racing to grow up and gain independence practically my whole life. My parents have videos of me at three asking a never-ending series of "why" questions until no more answers remained. I learned the word precocious at a young age.

Suddenly, adulthood felt like something to run away from.

Despite the lack of concrete action from this incident and the many similar instances since then, I still believe the first step to tackling injustice is to say something and to make known the unjust thing. There is power in naming it. But we then need to be prepared for the much harder and patient work of making the change happen.

Arfa opened my fifteen-year-old small-town eyes to a whole different set of experiences. She made me want to be an ally to her and others who experienced discrimination. She taught me, patiently, about her culture. Our friendship inspired a series of choices that eventually led me to meet my husband.

In fact, in her maid of honor speech at my wedding, Arfa took full credit for, as she put it, "being the reason for my happiness" on that day. She was not wrong.

Without realizing it, she helped set up a very different path for me to follow.

CHAPTER 3:

A DIFFERENT JOURNEY

"But your SAT scores are more than enough to get into University of Florida or Florida State," my high school guidance counselor said, seemingly flummoxed at my desire to go to school out of state, making sure to mention both schools given the intense sports rivalry. Few students each year went to colleges outside of Florida, so I forgave his confusion about my plan.

"Well, I have always wanted to go to school out of state and be in a city," I said. "Plus, I want to study international relations, and New York seems like the best place to do that." I had decided with certainty and limited information that I was going to study international relations in New York City, confidently believing I knew everything at the age of seventeen.

"I'm not sure what advice to give you but given your transcript you should be able to get in anywhere. If you need a recommendation letter, I'm happy to write one," he replied.

I did, ultimately, get accepted into New York University, one of only a few classmates to go out of state for school.

I had an almost romanticized idea of the city I used to only visit on special occasions with my family growing up. New York City felt like returning home and "making it" all at the same time. My friends and I often talked about our plans to get out of Flagler County and to do big things, as if the mere act of leaving was the end outcome. In some way, I felt like I already checked off a major life accomplishment.

When I realized I needed to focus on a geographic region and language as part of my intended International Relations major, I easily decided to focus on the Middle East and Arabic, inspired by hours of discussion with Arfa.

My previous experience with foreign language was two semesters of high school French where all I retained outside of *oui* was my zany French teacher's dramatic explanation of thinking about a calculator emitting perfume to remember that *la calculatrice* takes a feminine definite article. It took a lot of hubris given my background to tackle Arabic, one of the hardest possible languages, successfully.

I loaded up on as many classes about the Middle East as my scheduled allowed, trying to satiate my appetite to learn about the region. If anything, every class I took only increased my curiosity, making me want to learn more. Each class inspired new questions to be answered and new names of historical figures I had never heard of that barely colored in the picture of the culture that Arfa had outlined for me.

Sufism, Salah El-Din, Syria and Lebanon, the Mamluks and Fatimids, Rumi and Omar El Khayyam, and the discovery of "black gold." All new names, words, places, and concepts had books if not libraries written about them. Still, it was not enough. I needed to know more and to experience it all in person.

Which is how I came to be sitting on a plane in 2007, alone, to live a semester abroad in a country of eighty million, according to estimates by the World Bank at the time, where I knew not a single person but knew many facts. Cairo is the largest city, population of something growing close to 20 million by many estimates. Alexandria is the next largest city, located on the Mediterranean. The Pyramids of Giza were built roughly five thousand years ago. Egypt had been conquered by the Arabs in the seventh century. The Egypt of today had a Muslim majority population with a sizeable Christian minority and less sizeable Jewish minority. From the window seat on the last leg from Florida to Cairo, I only knew that I was leaving behind my small-town roots and trading streets that all started with "W," like some perverse episode of Sesame Street, for a city where I couldn't even read the street signs.

Studying abroad in Egypt seemed like a great idea and the only way to improve my Arabic skills and understand a culture I only had read about in books. I chose Egypt from a short list of potential study-abroad programs in Arabic speaking countries, inspired by both the pyramids and understanding that the Egyptian dialect is the most widely understood given the popularity of Egyptian movies and music. It was also an idea that I was seriously regretting at that moment. Despite all the planning, I spent little time thinking about what it would mean to actually live in Egypt.

How can you imagine or plan for something you have never done?

I could be in Italy right now eating pasta, I thought as I looked out the plane window and got more and more apprehensive about the eventual landing of the plane at Cairo International Airport.

I had stubbornly turned down an NYU-sponsored program in Italy with my closest friends to study abroad in a country alone, without any friends, and where I could barely speak the language. Because I wanted to learn Arabic. And see the pyramids. Right.

For once Catherine, I thought, *it would have been great to take the easy road.*

Deep down (really deep down at that moment), I felt excited about the adventure I firmly believed I would have. But on that final leg to Cairo, I could only feel nervous, anxious, and afraid.

The only person I had to rely on was myself. And that seemed terrifying.

I like to-do lists, spreadsheets, and workplans. When I don't know what to expect I think of all the myriad things that might happen and create many backup plans for imagined scenarios.

So that's what I did, while sitting in a cramped plane seat, I started planning for different scenarios. Or rather, worst-case scenarios.

What if the university shuttle didn't show up to take me to my university-rented apartment? How was I going to find the address? How would I make a phone call since my cell phone won't work when I land? Were there pay phones? Would there be a place to exchange US dollars to Egyptian pounds if I needed to get a taxi? Would there be taxis? Would anyone understand the Modern Standard Arabic I learned in school? Or would someone speak enough English for me to talk to if I didn't know where to go? What if I couldn't figure out how to leave the airport? What if I had nowhere to go?

I eventually decide that my ultimate back-up plan was to book a ticket to Florence, Italy and hang out with my two friends and spend the semester learning about European art history. *I can sleep on the floor of their apartment or something*, I thought.

I had taken several semesters of *fusha* (Modern Standard Arabic) and could very slowly and with a lot of concentration read Arabic script and write the most basic sentences like "I want water" or "I live in New York" — basically toddler-level Arabic.

I did not have a talent for languages, which my Lebanese Arabic professor made abundantly clear to me in class.

"Ya Catherine," he started when I told him about my idea to study abroad in Cairo, "you will not understand Egyptian Arabic. It will sound like a totally different language than *fusha*."

Right, I thought to myself, *as if I understand fusha either...*

"Egyptians may laugh at you for using *fusha,* it will sound like using Shakespearean English to ask for directions to the bathroom," he chuckled.

To prove him wrong, I filled out my application to study abroad at the American University in Cairo the next day.

I stubbornly proceeded with my study abroad plan. It was not until that moment on the plane, hearing this language spoken around me that did not at all sound like classroom Arabic, that I began to agree with my professor: *I might be in over my head.* The longer I sat there listening to the lightning-fast Arabic by my Egyptian plane-mates, as if my Arabic classes were a giant hoax to convince me that I was learning Arabic when actually they were teaching me Japanese. I couldn't understand one word. That's not true, the one word I could pick out was *la'a* (no) or the random assortment of English words sprinkled into what otherwise felt like Arabic soup.

Perfect, I thought. *If only my Arabic textbook Al Kitaab (the book) had taught me the word for "left" and "right" before I learned the translation for "United Nations," then I might have a chance.*

I knew that each Arabic speaking country had their own dialect, with some North African countries infusing French or Berber while other dialects like Egyptian or Gulf Arabic changed the pronunciation of certain letters. I would soon learn that Egypt also had different accents making Alexandrian and Cairene Arabic sound different too.

I am doomed, I thought. My hours of studying Arabic flash cards seemed farcical and misguided at that moment. What was I supposed to do, pull out a flash card to communicate?

Then suddenly, I overheard a conversation behind me that immediately made me feel as if I was not the only person foolish enough to board a plane alone to a country they had never visited before.

"Where do most students live who attend the American University in Cairo?" asked someone behind me.

"Most live with their families, but some of the students live in the dorms in Zamalek whose families aren't from Cairo," another person said. "I live with my family in a suburb in Southern Cairo called Ma'adi," he continued.

"Is Zamalek the neighborhood that is on an island in the Nile?" asked another person.

"Yes, it's only a short bus or taxi ride to Tahrir Square from there."

As I listened, I realized this sounded like a group of students also studying abroad at the American University in Cairo, one of whom seemed to be Egyptian based on his answers to the rapid fire set of questions. I ordinarily avoid talking to strangers on planes, but I felt so nervous about being totally on my own in a foreign country where I could barely put two words together that I did something very uncharacteristic and got up, went over to them, and introduced myself.

"Excuse me," I said, "are you also studying at the American University in Cairo?"

They all nodded.

"Oh, I'm so glad. No one else from my university is here and they put me in these Garden City apartments not the dorms, and I have no idea where that is or how to get there if the van that's supposed to pick us up isn't there, since my phone won't work, and I don't know how to make international calls, and I don't even know if I have the number for someone at the university, and I was getting so worried about not being able to know where to go, and I'm just so glad there are other people on the plane that are also studying at AUC," I said so quickly they probably barely understood more words than I understood of the Egyptian Arabic around me.

"Don't worry, I'll make sure you're able to find the university shuttle," said the Egyptian student, in what was one of my first experiences with incredible Egyptian hospitality. "And if it doesn't show up, I'll make sure to get you a taxi and explain to them the address of where you need to go."

Feeling infinitely better, I returned to my seat with a few new allies in this foreign country.

See, I thought to myself, *I could be a diplomat. All those international relations classes were already paying off.*

I spent the rest of the plane ride romanticizing what my semester in Egypt would be like. In my head, I would be walking confidently through the streets of Cairo, speaking flawless Egyptian Arabic that I picked up simply from absorbing the world around me and packing my head full of facts about the layers of Egyptian history.

My vision for my time abroad was something at the intersection of Emily in Paris meets Indiana Jones. It would be a toss-up for which was more unrealistic.

This vision was much more comforting than thinking I would wander alone, lost in a city of millions of people without a map, cell phone, or the ability to communicate with a majority of the population.

"Please buckle your seatbelts as we begin our initial descent into Cairo International Airport," the flight attendant said over the intercom.

I looked out the plane window eagerly and hoped to see the pyramids or some of the numerous places I would soon explore. I imagined background music playing inside my head to help narrate this part of the journey — something that sounded epic and dramatic to go alongside this pivotal moment where a young adult from a small town in the South lands in a totally foreign country ready to become culturally and linguistically proficient.

Instead, I saw nothing but non-descript orange-brown sand. It was a bit anticlimactic.

When we got closer to Cairo, however, I saw the seemingly endless rows of residential buildings following little semblance of a city layout. The buildings looked as if someone threw buildings from the sky, and wherever they happened to land, they stayed.

I saw the Nile for the first time. It created a blue open wound between the chaotic layout of the city.

Finally, on one of the loops we made around the city, I saw *the* Pyramids of Giza All the pictures I had seen of the Pyramids of Giza included a seemingly endless stretch of sand surrounding them, which made them seem remote from modern day civilization. Instead, the city, with its cacophony of buildings, went right up to the edges of the pyramids, seemingly threatening to swallow them in a tidal wave of unfinished apartment buildings.

Once we landed, I raced to find the other study abroad students I had made friends with on the plane and clung to them like a life raft. The airport felt old, as if I had gone back in time and traveled across continents and oceans. Everything felt a little worn down, dusty, and the navigation signs only sometimes were translated into English.

Thank God for pictures, I thought.

My need to use the restroom outweighed my fear of losing my new friends, and I made a quick pit stop at the bathroom, which, thankfully, used the universal symbol for a woman's bathroom. When I entered the bathroom, a woman wearing a navy-blue shirt and pants, seemingly a uniform, sat on a small stool, and handed me a tissue. She also had a little tray in front of her where several types of currency lay strewn in a pile.

Initially, I was confused about the entire set-up, but once I got into the stall and realized there was no toilet paper, the tissue in my hand made more sense.

I didn't have any Egyptian pounds yet but gave her a US dollar and used one of the few useful words I knew, *shukran* (thank you).

I caught up to the other plane passengers and followed them through the airport. I assumed all paths would lead to immigration. *Right again*, I thought when we got to immigration, *I am on a roll.* At the immigration counter, I got my first taste of Egyptian resistance to forming lines. Instead of forming a line where one person stands directly behind a person who has arrived previously, the entire plane swarmed the immigration kiosks. Some began gently and discreetly shoving each other to get to the front.

Those of us from line-forming countries were easily identifiable by the look of shock and confusion on our faces as we tried to assess this unfamiliar system and how we would participate. Our only saving grace was that the kiosk for non-Egyptians had the smallest crowd, so far fewer people created the pileup occurring at the other immigration windows. The next task was how to get the "visa" we were informed we needed prior to getting to the kiosk. It took a kind Egyptian who spoke English to explain that we needed to go to one of the thoughtfully placed banks lining the walls to pay the $20, in US dollars, get a "visa" sticker, and then give that sticker to the immigration officer to stick into our passports.

I got my sticker and entered the gaggle of foreigners hoping to get through the gates of Egyptian immigration.

"Why are you here?" the Egyptian immigration officer asked.

Because I'm too stubborn to simply have a nice, chill study abroad experience with my closest friends in Italy where I could eat pasta and drink wine every day, I thought.

"*Ana edris fii al-gam'a',*" I said in butchered Arabic while proud of myself for trying.

"What?" he replied looking confused.

"To study at the university," I relented, using English. It was my first failed attempt at using my classroom Arabic.

My passport was stamped, and I was officially in Egypt.

I walked into the baggage claim hall and was greeted with a uniquely Egyptian scene.

Instead of waiting for the bags to go around the baggage carousel, several airport attendants had taken all the bags and put them in a pile adjacent to the carousel, which meant a horde of people from our plane and others were crowding around the growing pile of bags. It was like someone put a pile of food near an ant hill, and, suddenly, there was a swarm picking it apart. To this day, I have no idea why they don't leave the bags on the carousel for people to pick up themselves.

I found myself (again) unsure of what to do. Do I dive in through this crowd of people to grab my bag? Do I wait patiently until someone lets me in? Do I just wait until everyone else has gotten their bag?

I ended up waiting on the edge of this mass of people until the crowd thinned. When I was sure I saw my luggage, I tepidly dove between a couple people and dragged out my two bags from the pile.

At least my bags arrived at all, I thought.

In the rush to figure out immigration and collect my bags, my anxiety about how to find the university shuttle had subsided. I thankfully found my fellow plane friends and the helpful Egyptian student, uneventfully found the university-provided shuttle, and made it to my downtown apartment — a short walk away from the now infamous Tahrir Square and the main American University in Cairo campus.

I had, in quick succession, experienced seemingly mundane and routine travel steps that were both familiar and completely foreign. Figuring out, quickly, how to adjust meant panic, stress, quick observation, often kindness from strangers, and eventually an attempt at mucking my way through an encounter. Those steps would be repeated over and over again during the coming months. I often felt like a toddler learning how to experience the world for the first time.

These moments felt like a test, as if I couldn't really claim to live in Egypt unless I figured out how to navigate a particular situation. These tests sometimes had helpful explanations in "Lonely Planet," like how to figure out the cost of an unmetered taxi ride, although more often they did not.

Very often, I survived because of Egyptian hospitality. A sympathetic Egyptian would see my shell-shocked or anxious face and patiently explain or show me how to do something.

Equally as often, I stumbled through an interaction, leaving the Egyptian on the other side equal parts amused and frustrated at my inability to do something painfully basic like ordering food in a restaurant or hailing a taxi.

I quickly realized Egypt had far more to teach me than a book of facts. The more I learned, the more it felt I didn't know.

The biggest thing I didn't know was that my life was about to change. I found myself not only on a different path but on a different journey altogether.

CHAPTER 4:

A SUBTLE PUSH

———

As I began my semester in Cairo, I believed two things. One, my time in Cairo would only last a semester. And two, that I knew a lot about Egypt and the Middle East.

I was wrong on both counts.

I knew studying abroad in Cairo would be totally different, but I expected there to be a handful of familiar experiences or things to help ground me. Like orange juice.

Growing up in Florida, oranges were home. Oranges were a comfort food and a taste-of-home food. A food equally as at home on the sidelines of kids' soccer games as upscale organic fruit stands. Peel it, slice it, cut it, squeeze it —there are ample ways to consume an orange.

One day before classes started, a fellow floor mate suggested we stop for fresh squeezed orange juice on the way to campus; she was our resident Cairo expert by virtue of having spent several weeks over winter break exploring the city and having command of a marginal degree of Egyptian Arabic under her belt.

She navigated us to a hole-in-the-wall juice stand I would not have realized existed. The stand had a tiny counter that housed a large juice-squeezing contraption with a hand crank;

fruit cuddled together in nets hanging from the ceiling. The man, who operated the store, barely fit in the space between the counter and back wall. His head grazed the back wall lined with shelves full of glass mugs. The juice man would grab an orange, cut it, turn the juice squeezer crank, and the fresh squeezed juice would pour into the waiting cup. Customers would stand at the counter and gulp down the juice before continuing with their day.

"*Ihna a'ayazeen a'aseer, law'sahmaht* (we would like juice please)," she requested, sounding like an expert to my untrained ears.

"*Mashy, khamsa* (okay, five)?" he responded, quickly counting up the number of foreign women taking up all the space at the counter and attracting attention from passersby.

"*Aiywa.* Takeaway *law-sahmaht* (yes, takeaway please)," she said. I caught only the word "takeaway."

The man stared at her. His eyes glanced at the glasses standing ready behind his head, clearly confused about why we weren't pausing with our walk to simply drink the juice at the counter. It had not crossed our mind to stop and drink the juice, we assumed we could multi-task our walk with a to-go container.

Clearly, this had not been the first time the juice man encountered overly impatient foreigners wanting to get their juice "takeaway" as he quickly shrugged, pulled out several plastic sandwich-sized bags that he poured the juice into, inserted a straw, and tied a rubber band around bag and straw.

I added drinking orange juice from a plastic bag to the list of ways oranges could be consumed.

Garden City, a neighborhood bordering Tahrir Square and home to numerous embassies, including the American Embassy, was designed by a French architect who was seemingly obsessed with circles; the neighborhood was made up of a set of concentric circles, which made it maddingly confusing to figure out how to navigate the tree lined streets.

Garden City itself was a bastion of quiet and peace compared to the near constant Cairo traffic. It was bounded on one side by the Corniche along the Nile and on the other side by Qasr Al-Aini street, a busy road that ran parallel to the Nile and a main thoroughfare. Going through the neighborhood quickly by car was almost impossible between the numerous embassy checkpoints and speed bumps, in addition to the odd curvature and intersections.

Once you exited the side streets, the chaos and vibration of the city smacked you in the face.

One of the first times I made the short walk from my apartment to the American University in Cairo with my three other roommates, the minutes were so filled with new sights, sounds, and adventure the stroll felt like an eternity.

We didn't have smartphones and the streets didn't have consistently clear or obvious street signs. Our route was based on directions from our apartment-floor security guard, who we thought had said to turn right once we got to Qasr Al-Aini (or "the really busy street" as we called it then). None of our Arabic was great so he could have been telling us to go to the moon.

Right felt as good a direction as any, so we went right. After ten minutes, we realized we were not correct and turned around to walk in the other direction.

Cars zoomed by us in no clear traffic pattern; the faint lane markers on the street seemed resigned to be ignored as cars, motorcycles, bikes, or pedestrians squeezed into every available space, like a moving Tetris board of vehicles. As if by magic this mass of moving vehicles and people were not immediately bumping into one another.

Meanwhile, we had our own obstacle course to navigate as we walked down the sidewalk strewn with potholes, electric wires, kiosks selling candy and soda, half-awake police officers leaning on their hopefully unloaded rifles, a missing paver here, and a trash heap there. Breaking through the car horns and traffic, a man pushing a cart down the street and yelling "*bekiya* (old used items)! *bekiya! bekiya!*" a call that would become so common to us that we would stop hearing it.

We passed the road that led to the U.S.Embassy and then reached the Mugamma, the central government administration building, that sat right on Tahrir Square; many of my Egyptian friends joked about how America was literally behind Egypt because the U.S. Embassy was located directly behind the heart of Egyptian bureaucracy.

We got to the last intersection before Qasr al-Aini spilled into Tahrir Square, which meant we had to cross the street to get to campus. I felt completely bewildered by how to get across the street with no visible crosswalk or traffic light to slow traffic. We watched for several minutes as cars sometimes whizzed and sometimes crawled their way into and out of the square. We saw a number of Egyptians run into oncoming traffic and make it across the street unscathed, weaving between barely moving cars or repelling cars as if by magic. Eventually, my roommates and I inched into the street. Four white women trying to cross a busy Cairo street attracted attention and an Egyptian, seeing our plight, showed us how to cross the street. The lesson I took away was to hope eye contact allowed me to win the game of chicken I played with each car.

I have to do this every day? Maybe multiple times a day? I thought. Crossing the street in Cairo felt like the most dangerous thing I had done up until that point in my life. There was no way I would survive.

And then, once safely across the street, the call to prayer began.

"*Allah akbar* (God is the greatest), *Allah akbar,*" came from every direction.

Observant Muslims pray five times a day: *fajr* before sunrise, *thuhr* around noon, *asr* mid-afternoon, *maghrib* right after sunset, and *isha* in the evening. Islam has five main pillars of the religion that are considered essential to practicing the faith; prayer is second only to confessing belief in *Allah* (God).

The timing of each of these five prayers changes over the course of the year with the rising and setting of the sun, but all the other rituals surrounding prayer remain the same: perform *wudu*, the cleaning of hands, arms, face, and feet, the laying of a prayer mat in the direction of Mecca, and then a series of standard supplications and prayers. While today many Muslims, especially those not living within earshot of a mosque, have apps or alarms set on their phones, historically, that job was left to each mosque. A *muezzin*, the person who calls the prayer, climbs the minaret attached to the mosque to recite the *adaan*, the words that make up the call to prayer.

The call to prayer, always recited in Arabic, can be beautiful and melodic when done by a talented *muezzin*. In Cairo, when I lived there, the task of calling the prayer often falls to recordings blasted from speakers with variable sound quality from the top of buildings or from people's cell phones.

At each mosque around the city someone or speaker begins blasting the call to prayer at roughly but not precisely the same time. No matter where you are in the city you begin to hear the rise and fall of the cadence of the *adaan*, like waves on the beach all crashing at slightly different intervals, making a combined and yet individual sound. That is what it sounds like to hear the call to prayer in the city of one thousand minarets.

It's like Cairo itself, the city with five thousand years of history, wakes up to speak in one voice with thousands of variations. Eventually, I did not even register that this was happening because it was part of the fabric of the city. This first time, however, we all stopped walking to listen. The sound was so arresting and all-encompassing.

In 2005, the Egyptian government decided the call to prayer needed to be standardized to create a unified and consistent sound across the city (Smith, 2005). Unfortunately, the power of the Mubarak regime was no match for the underlying stubbornness of a city thousands of years old. A 2010 headline in NPR declared "In Cairo, an End to the Cacophony of Calls to Prayer," following a law passed to attempt to bring order to the multitude of *muezzine* calls to prayer across the city. However, a popular magazine in Cairo Egypt Today reported in 2019 a pilot of sorts was just getting off the ground in a small subset of mosques across the country. Ultimately, however, there was not much progress in making change.

To me, it wasn't only the sounds that were new. Everywhere I looked I saw something I had never seen before — an entire extended family riding a singular motorcycle, an American fast food chain sign written in Arabic, Coptic Churches, endless minarets, palaces in the midst of barely finished apartment buildings, statues of well-known Egyptian historical figures unknown to me, and men riding bicycles with impossibly large trays of fresh baked bread balanced on their head; I'd come to learn these men often were transporting government-subsidized bread from central bakeries to stores for Egyptians to purchase. This bread was called *aish balady,* which translates to "traditional life."

There was one visual that once seen became impossible to miss, like finding Waldo. Ever present throughout the city, this image competed with the minarets for prominence. The image was of President Hosni Mubarak.

One of the facts loaded into my head before arriving in Cairo was that President Hosni Mubarak was the President of Egypt and had been since 1981 following the assassination of President Anwar Sadat. I vaguely knew the lineage of "modern" day Egyptian presidents. President Nasser had led the Free Officers in a coup that overturned the Egyptian royal family in 1952. A revolutionary, Nasser's rule was marked by a dream of Arab nationalism and communism, which included the government seizure of private property and nationalization of private businesses (Goldberg, Benin, 1982). President Sadat, a longtime advisor and fellow member of the Free Officers revolution, took power following Nasser's death. Despite their closeness throughout Nasser's presidency, Sadat took Egypt on a totally different trajectory. He opened the economy and, notably, became the first Arab President to sign a peace treaty with Israel following the 1973 War (Note: While also referred to as the Yom Kippur War, Egyptians refer to the 1973 war between Egypt and Israel as either the 1973 War or simply Sixth of October, a date used to name cities, streets, and bridges).

Mubarak, who had risen up through the air force, had become Sadat's Vice President after his successful leadership as commander of the air force during the 1973 War. He sat right next to President Sadat when Sadat was assassinated by Islamic extremists in a parade commemorating the war with Israel.

Mubarak inherited a set of challenges from Sadat including isolation from Egypt's Arab neighbors following the peace treaty with Israel — an unpopular move in both Egypt and the broader Arab community — high unemployment or underemployment, and an active Islamic extremist element within the country.

Unlike his predecessors, Mubarak was not a visionary or revolutionary. He was a believer in incrementalism. From the time he took power to the time I arrived in Egypt in 2007, he had taken enough small steps to address those three challenges. He had mostly repaired relations with Arab countries, made easier after Jordan similarly made official peace with Israel. He continued the path set by Sadat on economic liberalization, floating the Egyptian pound, investing in tourism, and increasing access to foreign direct investment. He also, after additional bloody attacks by a group called Gama'a al-Islamiya throughout the 1990s, cracked down on Islamic extremism, although not before several individuals who would come to carry out attacks against the US fled Egypt (Cook, 2012).

My personal introduction to Mubarak, however, was while trying to buy a snack in between classes from a corner store right outside the gates of the AUC campus. The cashier had resorted to a calculator to show me how much I owed after I failed at translating in my head the Arabic number he was saying; I thought he said the Arabic word for three, not eight. I fumbled with the Egyptian currency I had in my wallet, still a novice at sorting through which colored bills equated to which numeric values.

I finally produced the amount I owed, handed it to the cashier, and noticed a picture of a man standing in a suit, unsmiling, wearing aviators. I thought about asking the cashier who this smirking man was in the picture, but I did not feel confident my Arabic would get the question across much less that I would understand the answer.

Instead, I waited until back on campus to ask a fellow American classmate to avoid showcasing my ignorance.

"Hey, I saw a picture of a man in a suit in the corner store across the street just behind the counter. Do you know who that is?" I asked.

"Oh, you must mean President Mubarak," they replied.

"Really? Why would the small corner store have a picture of the President hanging up?" I asked.

"To show they support him I guess," they said.

"Why would they want to do that?" I naively wondered out loud.

My classmate shrugged.

Once I saw that first picture of President Mubarak, I saw his picture everywhere I went. He appeared in numerous tiny stores across the city, including at my now routine daily juice bar. He appeared taped to the dashboard of taxis. He appeared on billboards along the highways that chopped their way through downtown Cairo. He appeared on a giant banner hung from a government building. Seeing the decades-old picture of President Hosni Mubarak everywhere I looked was like the manifestation of the state always watching you, making sure you didn't step off the path of ardent regime support, much less ever believe another Presidential option possible.

It felt designed to scare away opposition and cement his power. Those citizens who chose to display a picture of the

President either wanted to ward off suspicion by the police of being anything but a regime supporter or signal an openness to accepting the economic spoils of political power.

* * *

In the classroom, I learned about the plausible theories of how the Ancient Egyptians built the pyramids, the musical chairs of rulers throughout Egypt's history, and how to conjugate Arabic verbs.

But most of what I learned was not in the classroom.

My Egyptian Arabic lessons came from riding taxis and trying to get from one place to another; I learned the word for "left" because I got lost one night coming home from a bar with friends and stopped to ask a security guard how to get home. I learned the names for fruit from Arabic juice menus and my vegetable vocabulary from pointing at squash and cucumbers huddled together in the neighborhood vegetable stand.

I also learned how to order Egyptian street food.

I had asked an Egyptian classmate, "What is a truly Egyptian dish I should try and where should I get it?"

"You definitely need to try *koshary*. Best place is Koshary Tahrir."

Koshary is a carbohydrate parfait, both cheap and filling. It starts with rice, then pasta, lentils, tomato sauce, fried onion, and is topped with a garlic oil sauce and, for the more adventurous, hot sauce.

My Egyptian classmate probably chuckled over the suggestion knowing both the chaos involved in ordering food from Koshary Tahrir and the likelihood I would get mild food poisoning from eating there so soon after arriving in Cairo. The relative absence of food safety standards meant that a certain amount of gastric discomfort and bouts of can't-move-from-bed food poisoning became expected and routine.

I coerced a fellow classmate to join me, and we set off to find Koshary Tahrir. Although Koshary Tahrir was practically around the corner from the university's campus, we got lost at least three times while trying to figure out whether we turned towards Tahrir Square or away from it, and then trying to be clever by taking a side street and ending up on a totally different *midan* (square).

When we finally arrived, I was embarrassed at how close it was and how long it took to finally find it, but the real adventure was figuring out how to order. The storefront was narrow with little room for customers to stand inside. Inside, there was no obvious menu, no place to make a line to order, and no obvious cashier. All we saw was a crowd huddled inside and spilled out onto the street. A man was behind the counter with several large pots of the key ingredients of *koshary* ready to make individual orders.

We had no idea how to get from having no *koshary* to eating *koshary*.

The standard process at any restaurant I had been to up until that point in my life was this: get in line, look at the menu, make selection to obviously designated cashier or wait staff, pay, and then receive food. This experience was missing most of those key process points.

So how do you order *koshary*?

After more than several minutes of observation, we deduced we first needed to go the man sitting on a stool in the corner, tell him what we wanted, pay, get a little hand-written paper, and then shove our way to the front of the crowd to give the paper to the man standing behind the counter making *koshary*.

What was a mystery, until a fellow Egyptian classmate saw our bewilderment and assisted in this process, was what exactly we were ordering beyond *koshary*, which was the exclusive thing the shop sold outside of bottles of water and soda.

We learned there were three options corresponding to different sizes: three Egyptian pound *koshary*, four Egyptian pound *koshary*, and five Egyptian pound *koshary*.

For the first of many, many times, I went up to the "cashier" and asked, *"Ana a'aayza khamsa koshary* (I want a five-pound koshary.)"

He wrote an Arabic "5" on a scrap of paper and gave it to me, while I tried to figure out how to get to the counter past a crowd of people similarly trying to get *koshary* standing in our way. We first tried to casually weave between the crowd packed shoulder to shoulder; once it became obvious that looking for a pathway through the crowd would leave us exactly where we stood for the rest of the afternoon, we began hesitantly and then forcefully shoving people in order to get to the counter.

I got the sense that many of the men smirked at my back as I bulldozed through the crowd. Who is this American girl trying to eat *koshary*?

That's how it felt a lot of the time early on in Egypt, whether it was trying to eat *koshary*, drinking orange juice, buying groceries, taking a taxi or performing any of the life routines that feel unremarkable and barely worth mentioning back home. Being in Egypt was like pushing against the tide just to get through the day.

While this experience was foreign to me at the time, it took going back to America to realize we aren't that much different — Americans just prefer to push others out of the way much more subtly.

CHAPTER 5:

A NEW LOVE

Egyptians often say about Egypt, "if you drink from the Nile you will always come back."

Although, they also warn you against literally drinking from the Nile to avoid spending the trip in front of a toilet.

So, a metaphorical drink. I must have drunk a gallon.

My study abroad experiences in Cairo checked all the boxes: academics, culture, language, personal growth. Check, check, check, and check.

I also fell in love.

And I met the man that would become my husband.

I learned thousands of years of history from how the pyramids were built to the multitude of layers of rulers in Egypt and the Middle East. I got a taste of my first dictatorship under the authority of President Hosni Mubarak. I got proficient enough in Egyptian Arabic to get myself from point A to point B with a detour to point C in the middle.

My friends and I experienced Egyptian nightlife. We went to bars where the only thing on the menu was five Egyptian pound (~$1USD) locally made Stella beer. We partied at hotel clubs and the infamous Cairo Jazz Club until the morning call to prayer.

I slept under the stars in the middle of the Egyptian desert near the Bahariya Oasis after enjoying a Bedouin meal and midnight walk through the desert. I ate fresh-caught fish in the Mediterranean city of Alexandria. I toured the Pyramids of Giza — and learned despite what movies might try to convince you, pyramids simply are dirty and smelled.

I crammed everything I could into those several months, assuming I might not return to Egypt, possibly ever.

With six weeks left until I said *ma'salama* (goodbye or with peace) to Cairo I tacked on one last adventure, but little did I know that it would last a lifetime.

I went on a date.

My husband, Mohamed, and I disagree about when we first met. He remembers seeing me for the first time during the club fair before classes started; I had stopped by the booth for the club he helped run with my roommate. His first impression of me were my ill-advised bangs that I had cut myself in my dorm bathroom shortly before arriving in Cairo in an attempt at starting a new life chapter, like a sitcom character in a new season.

However, I remember seeing him at the first meeting of the club. What I remember was the gaggle of girls that enthusiastically greeted him when he walked into a room (he denies this happened). We saw each other at least once a week at club meetings. Sometimes we would chat. Usually, we would acknowledge each other on campus. Occasionally, we would text.

I thought he was cute the whole semester but didn't know if that was reciprocated. In any case, I was leaving. Despite my imminent departure, with less than two months left in my study abroad semester, and weeks of encouragement from friends, I texted him. Worst case scenario, I thought, I would return to NYU and never see him again and never have to live with the embarrassment of rejection.

"Hey — know any good Egyptian movies? I want to see one before I leave," I texted.

"Yup," he replied.

"Any suggestions?"

"I want to see 'In the Heliopolis Apartment.' Want to go?" he asked.

"Sure, sounds fun," I replied, playing it super cool.

While I sent the first text, he still maintains our first non-date date was all his idea. We went with a couple friends, one of whom drove us to the movie theater. Shortly into the movie, someone's cell phone went off, and the guy picked it up and started talking. Instead of instant shushes, no one seemed to bat an eye. Several minutes later, someone several rows behind us similarly struck up a not very quiet conversation with the person sitting next to them. Clearly movie theater silence was not the norm in Cairo, which was great because Mohamed translated as much as he could so I could follow along. The movie turned into dinner, which turned into drinks, which turned into a late night at a Cairo club. Mohamed and I, after spending the entire semester exchanging only a handful of words, could not run out of things to say.

The next morning, I recounted the events of the night to my roommates.

"Right, but did you have a good time? Do you think he'll call?" one of my roommates asked.

"Best date I have ever been on, but I doubt he'll call," I replied.

"Why? I thought it was a great date?" another roommate said.

"I don't know. Guys are weird. And flaky. He knows I'm leaving soon so I'm sure he wouldn't want to get involved.

Plus, there are like a thousand girls around him all the time," I said, leaning heavily on my experience with the college dating scene in New York.

College guys were often incapable of texting or calling so I simply assumed he would be the same.

In what would become a long series of events where Mohamed would prove me wrong, my phone rang. I got up from the couch and went into the other room.

"Hey Catherine, it's Mohamed. What are you doing today? I was hoping to take you to dinner."

I have never been happier or more excited to be wrong.

Getting ready for that second date, I did not give much thought to whether it was a good idea to start dating someone when my time left in Egypt was quickly dwindling. Maybe it was because I didn't believe this could possibly turn into anything serious enough, quickly enough to matter; or maybe it was because Mohamed and I on paper were so different and lived so far apart that this felt like nothing more than another fun night; or maybe it was simply because I liked him so much after one date that I forgot to think about "the plan" for once.

If future Catherine had parachuted down to explain the future of Mohamed and I's relationship, I would have told her that I am far too rational and pragmatic for a story like ours to unfold. I had a plan for myself that involved another two years of undergrad, three years of law school, and then the rest of my life would begin. That plan did not leave much room for falling for an Egyptian guy who I likely would never see again.

Thankfully, future Catherine did not appear.

Mohamed took me to a restaurant called Estoril in downtown Cairo whose address is "off Talaat Harb Square"

— which meant that it was on a side pedestrian street. Finding places like Estoril was only possible if you already knew where it was. A food writer would not give it too many stars for the food, and a less informed travel writer getting their paragraph in on deadline would likely miss its significance. The smoke-filled restaurant included Egyptian dishes like falafel inhabiting the same neighborhood on the menu as savory crepes. The other diners were mostly Egyptian, unlike many upscale restaurants that cater to foreign tourists; this clearly was not a stop on a tourist map.

Estoril was part of a layer of Cairo often overlooked by both foreigners and many Egyptians. It belongs to a boxed set of restaurants and bars in downtown Cairo that Mohamed would soon introduce me to that represented a different era —an era when downtown Cairo was the place to see and be seen. It belonged to a time when Gamal Abdel Nasser and intellectuals, like the most famous Egyptian writer Naguib Mahfouz, frequented establishments like Café Riche, around the corner from Estoril, and downtown Cairo operated as a melting pot of ideas, cultures, and nationalities.

The great Egyptian writer Alaa Al Aswany described downtown Cairo through one of his primary characters in *The Yacoubian Building,* an international bestseller about the perceived decline of Egyptian society since the 1952 Revolution to the 1990s told through the occupants of the once prestigious Yacoubian Building in downtown Cairo:

"It was a different age. Cairo was like Europe. It was clean and smart and the people were well mannered and respectable and everyone knew his place exactly...I had my special places where I would spend the evening — the Automobile Club, the Club Muhammed Ali, the Gezira Club. What times! Every night was filled with laughter and parties and drinking and singing."

The haze of nostalgia on downtown Cairo's ornate buildings and storefronts created an illusion of the "good times" of an era now passed Of course, not all Egyptians could afford to see and be seen, even when downtown Cairo held that allure. Sitting there in the smoke-filled Estoril that history and understanding of downtown Cairo didn't exist for me yet. Downtown Cairo felt unfamiliar, the place I frequently got lost, struggled to understand, and a source of constant misunderstanding and mishaps. I was constantly stressed walking outside the gates of AUC, living in perpetual survival mode. That night was not about understanding Cairo but understanding Mohamed.

I learned Mohamed was born and raised in Cairo and lived his whole life in downtown Cairo.

Unlike most of the Egyptian students at AUC, it was not a foregone conclusion he would go on to study there; far and away the best university in Egypt, only a sliver of Egyptian high school students had the English language proficiency necessary to attend, the national test scores to qualify, and, most importantly, the ability to pay the tuition.

Mohamed, like many Egyptians, attended a private high school. His school did not come with the practical guarantee of getting into AUC like Egyptians who attended the more prestigious (and expensive) private schools. Most of his high school classmates ended up at either lower tier private universities or the massive public universities, made free to any Egyptian under President Nasser but doomed to be overcrowded behemoths with stretched-thin budgets.

To get into AUC, Mohamed studied and placed in the top 1% of Egyptian students on the national high school exam. His scores earned him entrance and a scholarship into AUC. Originally an engineering major, like in many countries one of a handful of "acceptable" majors, he decided to earn an Economics degree to follow his passion for finance and business instead.

We would come to discover how similar we were: stubborn and persistent in pursuing a goal, unafraid to say exactly what was on our mind, and fundamentally believed in doing things we were passionate about, sometimes despite easier paths.

On paper, Mohamed and I are nothing alike. We were born in different continents. He was raised Muslim, and I was raised Catholic. He grew up in an apartment in one of the largest cities in the world, and I grew up in a house in a somewhat rural area of Florida. I grew up in a democracy, and he grew up entirely under the rule of President Hosni Mubarak.

Sitting in the restaurant that night, it became clear how similar two people from totally different places could be, and how on paper differences were no match for an authentic connection, a romantic seedling.

After dinner, he suggested we take a walk around downtown. My ability to figure out where I was in downtown Cairo was still shaky at best. The spider's web of squares and streets, many with no obvious names, still felt impossible to navigate. This time, as we left the restaurant, Mohamed confidently led the way, and it was like I could finally see the city around me for the first time. I wasn't on edge trying to figure out if this street led to Talaat Harb Square or back to Tahrir. I didn't have to figure out if the corner store was the same one I passed five minutes before or if I had managed to find some totally new part of the city.

I could relax, take everything in, and see what Cairo looked like without freaked out, foreigner goggles.

He took me to an unmarked antique shop whose window was only partially visible on the street. The shop was below street level, another place only locatable if its location was already known. The shop was like stepping into the closet of a wealthy Cairene during the 1950s. Stacks and stacks of old Egyptian records, paintings of buildings in downtown Cairo, a mix of traditional Egyptian and Western furniture, decorative goods, and knick-knacks of all varieties filled the shop. Omm Kalthoum, an Egyptian icon from the 1920s through 1970s, sang in the background, her voice weaving Arabic poetry into song.

Mohamed knew the shop owner, who he quickly struck up a conversation that I could barely catch more than a vocab word here or there like *sharaa'* (street) or *midan* (square).

At the conclusion of the conversation, the shop owner brought out a box of old postcards and pictures of Egypt, which we began flipping through. Mohamed picked out an old postcard that had an image of the Pyramids of Giza and Great Sphinx of Giza. The postcard must have been decades old because the picture was before the Great Sphinx of Giza had been restored, its neck reinforced. He bought the postcard, wrote a message right there in the shop, and told me to read it later.

I initially was suspicious that this could all be too good to be true.

Over the next several weeks, Mohamed took me to place after place I had never been in and around Cairo. We went to shops and restaurants I would never have thought to look up or even realized existed. Although I had been to Khan Al Khalili, the open-air market dating back to Fatimids in the tenth century and a prime tourist destination, I had never bothered to cross the street to the "non-tourist" part of the market. When Mohamed said he wanted to take me to "the spice market" I had no idea what he was talking about.

He led me down a pedestrian street that seemed impossible to walk down given how packed it was with people, shops spilling into the street, and the occasional car or motorcycle that would insist on forcing people to press their backs against the walls to get by. The street, Al Mu'iz Street, led to Bab Zuwayla built in the eleventh century by the Fatimids as part of their walled city and one of the last remaining original gates. The "spice market" Mohamed referred to was off the square in front of Bab Zuwayla where spices were displayed like watercolors, breaking up the pungent smells of garbage. We then climbed one of the two minarets poking up from Bab Zuwayla like horns; sitting at the top of the minaret I got a view of the Gordian knot of small streets.

Before we began dating, Cairo was this foreign city I barely understood. Seeing the city with Mohamed allowed me to fall in love with Cairo in a way that allowed me to both appreciate the adventure and history while also understanding the normalness of how someone could live there and how the city could feel like home.

About two weeks after we went on that first date, Mohamed told me he loved me while we were cooking rice in my kitchen. I argued he could not already be in love; two weeks later, I said I loved him too.

We saw each other almost every day of those six weeks before I was due to leave Egypt, but we pragmatically broke up, thinking we would likely never see each other again. I had two years left at NYU, and it was too long and too far for us to reasonably stay together.

Only two months before I thought my semester abroad had provided everything I wanted. I had no idea that I could fall in love twice — with a boy and with a city.

Leaving Mohamed after accidentally falling in love was incredibly painful

I went back to the United States expecting that while we might write a few emails back-and-forth that would be that.

But again, I was wrong.

Through some combination of Facebook messages, emails, occasional Skype video calls, and handwritten letters, we stayed in touch. Mohamed, just beginning a hobby in photography that eventually turned professional for a time, would send pictures he took from around Cairo along with his handwritten letters.

Despite the feelings we had for each other and despite how serious it felt like our relationship could be, I thought it far more likely we would never see each other. But then, over the course of what became my last year in college, the economy of the US and much of the world took a nosedive.

My hometown in Florida turned out to be a canary in the coal mine as my parents' real estate business shriveled in early 2007 and took their hard-earned lifesavings along with it. We had no idea that my tiny county in Florida would foreshadow a set of economic events few predicted. In the fall of 2007, I decided to graduate a year early by cobbling together a Middle Eastern Studies major to save a year's worth of tuition and student loans. I sat in an Economics class in March of 2008, only a few months before graduation, and I saw the disbelief and shock on the faces of all the would-be investment bankers the day Bear Stearns fell. Because I decided to graduate early, I had not applied to graduate school per my original plan, so while I would be saving a year's worth of tuition, I had no plans for what I would do after graduation. There were few if any jobs to be found in the spring of 2008 for recent graduates.

As a result, I decided to move to Egypt, which somehow felt less risky than staying in America.

I bought a plane ticket to Cairo before I had a job lined up. I had enough money saved up from college jobs to last the summer if I didn't figure something out.

Mohamed was thrilled. I was equal parts thrilled and terrified — thrilled to be able to give our relationship a real chance and terrified of how to start my adult life in a totally different country with no job, barely any savings, and no backup plan. Again, I am thankful future Catherine did come to tell 2008 Catherine that this plan felt farfetched.

I went back to Egypt thinking it would be a gap year until I started law school. I never imagined or planned to stay any longer than that; even a year felt like a long time. I also thought my semester abroad had prepared me for the unexpected and the unplanned. I thought I had learned enough about Cairo and Egypt to know what living there would be like.

I was wrong...again.

CHAPTER 6:

A ROUTINE NEGOTIATION

———

My parents were perpetually late and, to rebel against them in high school, I insisted on being perfectly punctual. I buffered in extra time for travel to make sure I could be somewhere a few minutes early —unless I was trying to make my high school curfew, in which case I always cut it close.

In Egypt, time is seen as a rough guideline, an approximation for a plan. Like the Nile, a plan always flows in one direction but was not predictable in its course. Whenever I made plans with Egyptian friends or with Mohamed, I budgeted a healthy buffer between when we agreed to meet and when they showed up.

Mohamed affectionately calls this "Egyptian Standard Time."

My friends and family back home sometimes asked whether the differences in our religion or country of origin caused issues in our relationship. If they did, they paled in comparison to our temporal beliefs.

"What time are you getting here?" I'd ask. "You said we were meeting at 7PM and now it's 8:30."

"I'm on my way," he'd say.

"'I'm on my way' isn't a time or timeline," I'd reply, knowing "on my way" could mean many events stood in the way of him arriving. It could mean he was beginning to think about getting ready, then needed to eat, talk with his family, run an errand, and then if the traffic allowed, pass by.

He'd show up at 10 PM.

Some Egyptian friends blame this time fluidity on the awful traffic in Cairo, while others explain it away as a simple cultural difference; Americans see a specified time as a rule, Egyptians see it as a suggestion. An Egyptian friend once explained the sequence of activities mattered not the time they happened. This explanation confused my time-sensitive brain.

Mohamed's theory is being timely creates additional stress and why create more stress? So really, being late is simply good self-care. He would like me to tell you he is (almost) always on time now.

It is laughable that I thought five months of studying abroad in Cairo would have revealed all the complexities of Cairo's culture or completely prepared me for the numerous mundane tasks and activities one must complete. Cairo has her own way of doing things, constantly changing and shifting her course.

Cairo in some shape or form has existed for nearly five thousand years.

Over the millennia before the Aswan High Dam was built in southern Egypt, the flooding of the Nile would alter the exact route and placement of the river each year. At one point, it is believed the Nile, during its annual flood, ran close to the Pyramids of Giza, enabling large stones of granite used in parts of the pyramids construction to float upriver from Upper (southern) Egypt. While the Nile is now more than five miles away, the city of Cairo has metastasized all the way to the entrance of the Giza pyramids; the city is now what is overflowing.

While the Aswan High Dam may have tamed the Nile, nothing to date has tamed Cairo from growing, morphing, and evolving.

So when I moved to Egypt in the summer of 2008, I had another year of formal Arabic, still largely useless on the streets of Cairo, and little more than what I called "study abroad Arabic." *Yalla* (let's go), *la'a* (no), *yameen* and *she-mal* (right and left), *belzabt* (exactly), *ishta'a* (cream or cool), *shukran* (thank you), *aiywa ba'a* (hell yes), and everyone's favorite, *mesh mushkila* (no problem). I even picked up the ubiquitous *ya'any*, which literally translates to "I mean" but is used similarly to how American use the word "like," peppered in between sentences indiscriminately. My vocabulary allowed me to get from one place to another, provided everything went smoothly, which almost never happened.

In those early months, without the oversight of a university program to help navigate, I relied heavily on Mohamed and my American roommates to figure things out. My roommates taught me where to get a haircut, how to find a local dry cleaner, and how to order groceries for delivery (it was far before the advent of smartphone-enabled delivery apps).

When I first arrived in Cairo, neither Mohamed nor I knew how long I would live there. Neither of us knew how long we had to develop our relationship, how long it made sense for me to stay in Egypt before going to graduate school, or whether I would even be comfortable living in Egypt. Continuing a relationship in these conditions, on top of all the additional cultural and temporal differences of opinions, tested our commitment to each other even early on. So, we took it one day at a time.

Mohamed continued to take me to new places in the city. We often would meet up with friends at Cairo rooftop bars, providing a brief respite from the constant crowds and noise of the street. We drank fresh juice or Egyptian beer while munching on *tirmis* (lupini beans) and sharing a *sheesha* around the table. Sometimes our group of friends would sit in an *ahwa* (coffee shop) whose patrons would spill out onto the streets sitting at wooden tables and chairs while drinking *shay* (tea) and playing *tawala* (backgammon).

I tagged along as he developed his photography hobby. He took pictures around the city from the City of the Dead to Coptic Cairo and from the Citadel to an average street in Mohandiseen. I continued to see the city with him as I also saw his literal perspective of Cairo through his photographs. We also traveled around the country together and with friends: we climbed Mount Sinai in the middle of the night to catch the sunrise at the top, got our scuba diving certification together in Dahab, slept overnight under the open air, went for desert walks at night, and traveled to the oasis of Siwa, one of the many rumored burial places of Alexander the Great.

Eventually, he introduced me to his parents and his siblings, which was considered a big step in Egypt. His family has always been nothing but warm and accepting of me, however early on they may have wondered whether our relationship would last given the hurdles in front of us.

Being in a romantic relationship without a formal engagement was not socially acceptable or common outside of the sheltered world of AUC. I didn't understand this at first because I often saw young men and women sitting at coffee shops or walking over the Qasr al-Nil bridge together, seemingly unmarried. Mohamed had tried to explain to me the careful nuance between "having" a relationship and "being" in a relationship and between meeting up publicly for coffee and dating sometimes behind closed doors. While studying abroad, I had a vague sense of the perceptions by Egyptians of dating a foreign woman, namely the assumption that it was primarily a physical relationship. Mohamed's friends were completely accepting and understanding of our relationship, so I initially was insulated from experiencing this stereotype. Every once in a while, it would smack both of us in the face.

One time, Mohamed and I were visiting a historic site in Cairo. Most historic sites have separate prices for Egyptians and foreigners, however Egyptian tour guides need special permission to give tours. We showed up at the ticket booth together and the person behind the counter asked Mohamed, "*Anta murshid* (are you a guide)?"

They began a back-and-forth in rapid Arabic. I mostly didn't understand. However, I did understand that Mohamed was getting increasingly upset.

He broke away to explain to me what was happening.

"He won't let us in because he thinks I'm a tour guide, and I don't have the proper paperwork," Mohamed said.

"Why in the world would he think that?" I asked.

"He doesn't understand how we could just be friends hanging out together," he replied. "Or that we were together but not married."

Mohamed and I tried our best to treat this as white noise and, instead, to focus on our relationship, while I figured out Egypt.

* * *

Cairo quickly taught me that everything, labeled price or not, was negotiable. The price of this chicken? Negotiable. Can we enter this restricted area of a historic site? Negotiable. The price of a taxi ride? Negotiable and, likely, arguable too.

Almost anything could be accomplished with a good discussion.

Past the touristic paraphernalia of Khan Al-Khalili through a crowded forest of buildings some hundreds of years old, one enters an area called Attaba where Egyptians come to shop for clothes, housewares, gold, and silver. Navigating the area takes an openness to getting lost (at least for me) and a willingness to share a small space of road with people, motorcycles, cars, donkeys, and fruit stands. Some vendors may list prices for some items, but, often, negotiation is required to reach an agreed upon price. This is where I tried my hand at haggling over prices and tried out my still growing comfort with Arabic numbers.

"*Law'sahmat, bikam* (excuse me, how much is this)?" I'd ask the person who appeared to be the vendor owner or worker.

"*Ashreen junayh* (twenty Egyptian pounds)," they would reply.

I'd spend a few seconds processing the number the vendor replied with. I translated it in my head into English before deciding on my counteroffer and then selected the correct Arabic number, like an early computer with a slow processing time.

"*Aashara* (what about 10 Egyptian pounds)?" I'd counter, knowing that the "foreigner" price was usually vastly inflated.

At that point, either they would counter or simply say "*la'a (no)*." Sometimes they might wait until I turned to walk away to shout out a counteroffer, testing my resolve.

Numbers were among the first set of words I internalized in Arabic. They were the first things I could say without constantly translating into English and then back to Arabic. The only way to gain enough credibility was to negotiate something less than the "foreigner" price for items.

I learned to negotiate the prices of basically anything, and I quickly learned the market prices for everything from tomatoes to cheese. I knew the cost of a bottle of water, the standard taxi fare to work, the price of admission to a night club, and even a hotel room when I traveled outside of Cairo. While I graduated from novice to proficient, watching Mohamed and his friends in action set the bar high for what negotiating mastery looked like.

Egyptians have a saying *"taa'ashrab shay"* which is a condensed version of the phrase *"taa'aala ashrab shay* (come drink tea)."* It is a way of asking a person to have a casual discussion before getting into the business of discussing business. While sometimes this meant drinking tea first, often it entailed an extended opening conversation before diving into the specifics. I would hear Mohamed start a negotiation asking how the person was doing and exchange an entire set of details about the person's life before ever asking for their initial price.

Years later in business school, I learned concepts like "ZOPA" (zone of potential agreement) and "BATNA" (best alternative to negotiated agreement). I almost laughed out loud at the idea of needing to be taught these fancy business terms for what many Egyptians did instinctually.

Sometimes, living in Egypt felt like one long, constant negotiation.

* * *

There are certain human characteristics that remain the same no matter the culture or country: love, anger, fear, hope — and a belief that the traffic is awful and worse than anywhere else.

Everyone else in the world is wrong unless you live in Cairo.

Cars filled every nook and cranny of the road. Lane markers, if they existed, were resigned to being ignored. Often, drivers drove so close together a driver could reach into a neighboring car to borrow a tissue from a dashboard tissue box.

The traffic was relentless. My short commute from my downtown apartment to my office along the Nile at the north end of the city could take fifteen minutes without traffic, but with traffic it could take upwards of an hour. The commute once took ninety minutes, which included walking the last mile because the traffic was so unbearable.

Cairo is not a city that lives by the rules. To survive, Egyptians resort to humor, like one of my favorite jokes about Egyptian driving:

An Egyptian taxi driver moves to a Western city. He picks up a passenger. The passenger says, "I'm in a huge rush I need you to drive quickly!"

The Egyptian driver says, "Don't worry, I'm a very good Egyptian driver!" He drives along, sees a red light, and speeds through it.

The passenger says, "What are you doing?! That was a red light!"

The driver says, "Don't worry, I'm a very good Egyptian driver!" He continues driving, another intersection, another red light, and speeds through it.

The passenger says, "That was another red light! You are going to get us killed!"

The driver says, "Don't worry, I'm a very good Egyptian driver!"

He continues driving, sees a green light, and stops.

The passenger says, "What in the world are you doing? The traffic light is green! The other cars have a red light, go!"

As the passenger finishes his outburst, another taxi comes flying in front of them.

The driver turns to the passenger and says, "See, another very good Egyptian driver."

The rules of the road, not unlike Egyptians' relationship with time, were subject to negotiation. Egyptian drivers operated under a social contract about how to navigate Egyptian streets, and it was different from the contract enforced in other countries by stop signs and traffic lights. Egyptians had to rely on each other because the government did not exist to enforce anything close to a traffic rule.

This social contract extended to directions. Sometimes when I got in a taxi, I knew the directions to my destination but much more often I did not. While difficult to imagine a world without an instant map complete with navigation, that did not exist yet for Egyptian taxi drivers (or me).

Instead, I would give a general destination or landmark the driver would likely know.

"Dokki," I yelled at a passing taxi that didn't look like anyone was sitting in the backseat.

The driver slowed done, not quite stopping, and motioned to get in. Once I got into the car the taxi driver, already shooting off down the street, turned and asked, "*Fayn fil Dokki law'samahat* (where in Dokki, please)?"

"*Midan Mesaha* (Mesaha Square)," I'd say.

If he knew the area well, he would ask "*Fayn fil-Midan Mesaha bezabt* (where in Mesaha Square, exactly)?" If he didn't know the area and I didn't either it was no problem. He would slow down to someone walking down the street once we got close and yell from the window, "*Law-samahat, fayn Midan Mesaha hadratik* (please, where is Mesaha Square, sir?"

If we were close by, the person would give some quick directions. If we were not at all close to where I was trying to go, the person might come over and give extended directions followed by arm motions to underline a point. If we were far off, the taxi driver might repeat this exercise several times until we arrived. It never was the case that a taxi driver gave up trying to figure out where I was going or that the person they asked for directions turned down their request; on many occasions this informal network rivaled anything a tech company could produce on an app.

* * *

When I first arrived in Egypt metered taxis did not exist. The only taxis were black taxis that often predated my years on earth — and seemed to be in competition with Cairo's millennia of history. While some taxis spewed exhaust, other taxis' backseats were so threadbare I could feel the metal undergirding the upholstery. Often, the meters were nothing more than a decoration like the multitude of mirrors often attached to the windshield or dashboard.

The lack of a meter meant haggling over the price of the ride at the outset, not knowing what kind of traffic we might experience on the way, knowing the "right" cost of a ride, and handing that amount to the driver at the end of the ride. Knowing the market rate for a taxi ride was like knowing the price for carrots or apples, it was common knowledge. Going downtown to Heliopolis? Twenty Egyptian pounds. Going downtown to Zamalek? Seven to ten pounds. Going downtown to Ma'adi? Twenty to twenty-five pounds (all prices circa ~2009).

Taxi drivers in Egypt had a mythology surrounding them. Yes, their primary task was to keep at least one hand on the steering wheel, one foot frantically switching between the gas pedal and the brake to avoid collision, and, hopefully, arrive at the stated destination. However, taxi drivers were also storytellers, political commentators, keepers of the miscellaneous facts, and unbelievable tales. They were entertainers on long slow crawls through Egyptian traffic and purveyors of passenger's life stories.

They also needed to be skilled mechanics to frequently fix the often broken-down vehicles they relied on to do their work; taxi drivers held onto their cars for so long that Egypt passed a law in 2008 outlawing licenses of taxis over 20 years old, which caused an outcry from drivers. The law also packaged a series of fines for violations like "speeding, eating and drinking while driving, or having a baby in the front seat," according to an article in Reuters "Egypt Wants Antiquated Taxis Off its Roads." When asked though whether new rules would keep Egyptian taxi drivers from running red lights (note: I don't remember ever seeing a working traffic light in Cairo) or speeding or keeping their antique cars on the road, a taxi driver in the article summed it up best: "It won't work for sure...everyone plays with the law here."

It certainly was laughable that a mere law could create order on Egyptian streets or amongst the taxi drivers who ruled the roads.

Khaled El Khamissi's 2006 best-selling book *Taxi* was a collection of short essays about stories told to him by drivers through countless taxi rides. They are stories that spoke to the numerous truths about Egyptian society. The stories documented in his book include how drivers struggle to pay for an education while using the free public school system, joke about the known-to-be-rigged elections, comment on democracy, and find it impossible to make enough money to pay their car loans while also saving enough to pay the inevitable bribe to a police officer.

"The difference between us [Egyptians] and them [US] isn't in democracy...but the difference is in the law. They have laws that are enforced, while we don't," one story recounted while describing a parliamentary election that in the taxi driver's view had wiped out the opposition to the National Democratic Party.

Even election outcomes could be negotiated.

Frequent fender benders turned into negotiations because car insurance did not exist. The only insurance while driving was that the plodding traffic would usually prevent any major damage. Often, the two drivers would get out of their cars, look at the two cars, and if there was little more than a dent or scratch, shrug their shoulders and get back in their cars. Sometimes, when the damage totaled more than a ding in the car, the drivers would negotiate, and often argue, which drew crowds of people to watch the spectacle.

* * *

While Cairo offered plenty of nightlife options, sometimes we needed a small escape from the city.

One of our regular activities was taking a *felucca* (Egyptian sailboat) out on the Nile for a couple hours. The *feluccas* were all lined up next to each other at a pier near downtown, each was independent from one another, and each had its own captain who would take us out. The *feluccas* could fit up to about ten to fifteen people. There were no motors. Instead, they were reliant on the wind to take us across the river and back. The *feluccas* were made of wood, completely flat, with wooden benches and colorful cushions lining either side of the boat.

The *felucca* captain, who almost always wore a traditional *galabiya*, a long shirt that went almost to the floor, and a scarf around their neck or head, would sit in the back of the boat to steer, practically level with the water. He would deftly maneuver the sail lines to change the direction of the boat.

We would typically go with a group of friends and bring food, wine, and, often, a guitar to enjoy as we cruised around the Nile. Taking a *felucca* ride after work gave us a break from the constant noise of traffic, the layers of smells that come from a city of nearly twenty million people, and the pollution that often made it difficult to take a deep breath. In the middle of the river, it was possible to forget we were in a city at all.

My Egyptian friends often warned me against attempting to swim or otherwise interacting with the Nile water as many people upriver would throw trash and refuse into the water. When I was on a *felucca*, however, the water seemed like a refuge from the chaos of the city.

The only sound that might overwhelm the sound of the river bumping against the boat was the sound of "party boats." These were motorized flat boats, low to the water, which fit thirty to forty people. They often had neon lights on the roof of the boat, and always blasted *shaabi* which was local folk music. *Shaabi* music is often heard at Egyptian weddings or in microbuses, part of the sound of the Egyptian street. At street weddings, it can be accompanied by the sound of *zaghrouta*, an exclusively woman-led ululation, expected at any Egyptian celebration.

While *shaabi* music has been around for decades, a more recent electronic evolution of *shaabi* music called *mahraganat* (festival music) entered Cairene ears in the mid-2000s. The music mixes traditional *shaabi* drums and instruments with electronic beats, rap, and catchy melodies. To me it simply sounds like fun, a party and is almost impossible to not dance to. The lyrics sometimes touch on politically and socially sensitive topics, and after a 2020 concert when a popular *mahraganat* singer referenced alcohol, the government-run Musicians Syndicate banned the entire genre of music from being performed in the country. The head of the Musicians Syndicate defended the decision by pointing to the singers' often lower-class backgrounds and "poor" voices according to reporting by the British Broadcasting Corporation (BBC). Of course, bans on art whether music, books, or film often serve only to make them more popular by giving them even greater attention.

Cairo was a vibrant, alive, and fun city.

It did not take long for me to realize though that *felucca* rides, nights spent on rooftop bars, and even having friends who owned air-conditioned cars to drive around the city instead of relying on the cobweb of formal and informal bus and microbus networks were not the typical experiences for most of the population. I slowly began understanding the gap between the world most of my Egyptian friends and I lived in. We lived in a world where we could go out to eat, drink and travel without thinking, and the world many, if not most, Egyptians did not inhabit; those spaces may occupy the same physical place on a map but were worlds apart.

The gap in these worlds caused frayed and open nerves. How would it feel to barely provide the basics to your family while people like my Egyptian friends and I were able to comfortably enjoy ourselves?

I didn't know it at the time, but these crumbling nerves within Egypt would soon be too much for Egyptians to tolerate.

CHAPTER 7:

AN UNTAPPED POTENTIAL

———

I realized I achieved a level of proficiency over living in Cairo when my parents and youngest brother came to visit.

As a study abroad student, crossing busy streets with no light to stop traffic terrified me. To catch a taxi home from work, I needed to cross what would have been a six-lane highway, if lanes existed, to avoid going a mile or more down the road before backtracking. I developed, slowly, an instinct to judge how far the cars were and how quickly I needed to scoot lane by lane across to the median before repeating the process; my roommates and I often compared crossing streets to the video game "Frogger." Egyptian drivers were accustomed to pedestrians intersecting busy roads but still expected street-crossing awareness from pedestrians.

My parents and brother had come to visit my office so I could give them the full picture of my life in Cairo. We walked out of the building after the tour and looked to me to give directions on our next step.

"Okay, so we're going to cross the road so we can hail a taxi," I said. "We'll go directly to the restaurant to meet Mohamed. Our reservation is now but likely some people will be late." Take that Egyptian Standard Time.

"Sounds good," they said. None of them had been to the Egypt or the Middle East before so I tried to give them the full experience and allow for plenty of time for them to get to know Mohamed. This trip was the first time they met him after years of me talking about him.

I briefly explained the way to cross the street and began darting out into traffic. I realized halfway across the road they were not following me. I looked back, and my dad was gesturing for me to come back.

"Cat, what in the world were you doing? I thought there was a crosswalk somewhere. There is no way we can cross the road this way!" he said.

Crossing a road with cars whizzing by had become so routine I practically forgot it was in any way abnormal coming from the US. I hailed us a taxi and tried to be okay with taking an extended ride instead of simply crossing the street.

Thankfully, my parents approved of Mohamed far more than my running out into traffic. By the end of the trip, they invited him to come for the Christmas holidays later that year.

* * *

Egyptians refer to Egypt as "*Om El Donya* (mother of the world)," which was a reference to Egypt's uniquely long and ancient history. This label does not take much convincing when remnants of Egypt's past are interlaced with its present. The first time Mohamed visited America, I tried to impress him by first taking him to New York City and showing him the sites. We saw a Broadway play, stood at the base of the

Empire State Building, and visited the Statue of Liberty and Ellis Island. I tried to explain the importance of Ellis Island and how some of my ancestors passed through on their journey to America.

"So when was Ellis Island opened?" he asked.

We found a helpful explanation of the history. He began looking unimpressed.

"What's wrong?" I asked.

"The mosque across the street from my house is centuries older," he said. Clearly, the almost 1900s barely counted as "history" to someone who grew up around five-thousand-year-old pyramids.

Egypt's ancient history and place in the world is certainly a source of pride and a distinct part of Egyptians' national narrative. However, it would be difficult to rely on Egypt's power from centuries or millennia before to inspire a population or to keep them believing in the current day ruling class. The everyday person does not feel motivated or safe because of history but rather because of the present. People want to feel safe, protected, and have hope for the future. Without those key ingredients, the bread of a country's opportunity would not rise.

The modern-day story Egypt tells itself, to me at least, is one of military might and victory, and strength and national pride in being Egyptian. The Egyptian flag is proudly waved at sporting matches and national celebrities, actors, and singers famous across the Arab world are showcased as symbols of Egypt's current cultural success. I often heard friends say "*Ana Masry* (I am Egyptian)," proudly and often.

This narrative is reinforced from the moment one exits the Cairo International Airport.

One of the first sights from the window of the taxi is a long mural on the wall of the Egyptian Military Academy.

The mural paints a picture of Egyptian military conquests and key military figures since the Free Officers movement in 1952. Faces of military leaders painted in larger-than-life proportions can be seen looking stern and heroic as they lead the two-dimensional soldiers and weaponry.

This message was reinforced through symbols and traces of military might littered across the city. Numerous bridges, streets, and a Cairo suburb bore the name "Sixth of October," the beginning of the War of 1973 of Arab countries against Israel that led to Egypt regaining control of the Sinai Peninsula.

President Mubarak, like the previous two presidents before him, came from the military. He was a war hero rising through the Egyptian Air Force. The military could become a career path but was also an obligation for all men as a partially conscripted armed force, Egyptian men upon exiting high school or university had to go through a military service lottery.

Egypt's military is a source of pride and a historical feeder program into the presidency; it also receives roughly $1.3 billion in military aid annually from the United States to purchase US military equipment as set forth in the 1979 Egyptian Israeli peace treaty: "an investment in regional stability, built primarily on long-running military cooperation and sustaining the treaty" (Egypt: Background and U.S. Relations, 2021).

Generally, the Egyptian military was well-respected and regarded within Egyptian society as a protector of the country, unlike its security cousins the Egyptian National Police or the dreaded Al-Amn al-Markazi (Central Security Forces). Both were known for their brutality against Egyptian citizens and the source of "disappearances" of political dissidents.

The Egyptian military was much more than a military. The Egyptian military owns and runs businesses that produced an array of consumer goods, created infrastructure, and owned large plots of land. Estimates put military control of the economy from anywhere between fifteen to forty percent in 2012 (Tadros, 2012). But also, between five and sixty percent (Hauslohner, 2014). The estimates vary because the military would prefer for the precise number to remain an estimate.

Investment in the narrative about Egyptian military might and prowess created a cornerstone for the overall Egyptian narrative while religion, with the blanket of mosques and churches, would certainly be another. How much of this narrative is simply a useful story to keep a population united? What does this story cover up?

In 2009, President Obama decided to visit Egypt and make a big speech in front of a crowd of Egyptian students at Cairo University. Egyptians generally were thrilled. One time, shortly after Obama had won the 2008 election, my landlord had come to my apartment to collect the monthly rent like he always did. Him and his wife sat down on the couch as I served tea, and we had our typical broken Arabic and English conversation.

"Obama *faz al-intikhabat* (won the election)," he said.

"*Aiwa*," I said.

He pulled out a picture from his pocket. "*Bussy, ibny sheklek zay Obama* (look, my son looks like Obama)!" he exclaimed.

That reaction sums up why many Egyptians were excited to welcome President Obama to Cairo. The day he arrived, most office workers across the city were given the day off, people were told to stay off the streets, and Egyptians crowded into *ahwhas* (coffee or tea shops) to watch President Obama's speech at Cairo University.

I have no idea if President Obama's security team realized this, but the route President Obama's motorcade would drive was obvious before his arrival —buildings were given a facelift all along the route. Crumbling apartment buildings were given a fresh coat of paint and trees and flowers were planted where there had never been trees or flowers before. I could have predicted his exact route by a trail of petunias.

Certainly, this provides evidence of Egyptian hospitality, which I encountered often whether it was someone kindly offering to walk me to my destination when I stopped to ask for directions or people handing out cups of juice for people sitting in traffic to break their fast during Ramadan. However, it also felt totally performative. It made me wonder what it said that the Egyptian government had the capability of "freshening up" but not the willingness on an ordinary day or for ordinary people.

Sometimes, the incessant flag-waving and obsessive patriotism is intentional to frost over what lies underneath and cover the struggles and cracks in the ground. For those who have little in the way of economic stability, this intense national pride either succeeds in creating the belief that they are part of the narrative or creates a feeling of exclusion.

Regardless, the gaps in the system exist.

Egypt's demographics, like many of its neighboring Middle Eastern countries, include a sizable young population. Estimates put over 50% of the population at under twenty-five years old and less than 5% over sixty-five years old (World Population Review, 2019). According to the U.S. Census Bureau, the US population under twenty-five is closer to 30% and over sixty-five a little above 15%. Numerous other factors fueled frustration and tension among Egypt's younger generations including high rates of youth unemployment or underemployment, the inability for many to marry given the expectation that men provide an apartment, and the cultural norm prohibiting pre-marital physical relationships.

I learned this partially from my Arabic teacher's selection of a particularly powerful book written about Egyptian society.

My teacher, Nour, gave Arabic lessons to make an extra income to supplement her husband's, while allowing her the flexibility to also raise her three children. Nour took her teaching very seriously, wanting to educate about both the language and the culture. She often selected Arabic songs or text that allowed us to discuss societal topics. She frequently supplemented these texts with her own real-life experience and described her experience being an Egyptian woman and parent to fill out the picture for me while I struggled to follow along.

She knew about Mohamed and I's relationship and sometimes tried to help explain a particular difference that I was struggling to understand. This was probably why she chose the book A*ayza Atgawiz* (I want to get married) by Ghada Abdel Aal for us to read together. Abdel Aal writes about her numerous potential marriage suitors or that of her friends in their quest to find a suitable husband. The book covers the incredible pressure put on women to simply pick a husband and the pressures, obstacles, and hilarity in finding suitors that can provide an apartment and demonstrate the ability to provide for a family. The book, written in colloquial Egyptian instead of the usual Modern Standard Arabic, weaves humor with the author's own anxiousness and insights to paint an often unseen picture.

The book, started as a blog and has sold hundreds of thousands of copies globally and, eventually, was turned into a hit TV show in Egypt, which is a good indicator of the relatability of her experience (Yaqoob, 2011).

The book also caused controversy and discussion in Egypt. Abdel Aal tackles numerous "off limits" topics like police brutality and dating but also flips the script by taking control of her own narrative. In Egypt, many Egyptians find their spouse through *gawaz al-salonat* (living room marriage), which is short-hand for an arranged marriage. This typically involves young suitors visiting a potential bride's apartment and going through something akin to an interview with varying degrees of control by the bride over the circumstance; the potential bride also has varying degrees of control over the final decision as typically her father or male relatives have final say. If the match goes forward, the male relatives will typically then negotiate the "financial provisions" like the apartment the groom is expected to supply.

In Egypt, mortgages were practically non-existent. This fact was coupled with a housing shortage made home ownership a distant dream for many young Egyptians. The lack of mortgage financing was one more example in a multitude of examples that held Egyptians back from hope of a different kind of economic future.

* * *

The American University in Cairo used to straddle three different campuses all within a block from one another on and around Tahrir Square. The main campus fronted Tahrir Square and included the iconic AUC building used in marketing brochures while the other two campuses were a couple blocks from the square and included more nondescript buildings, albeit clearly differentiated from the surrounding city by looking more modern and well-kept; AUC itself was out of bounds for much of the population to access, the closed campus reinforced reality.

Across from AUC stood the Mugammaa, the main Egyptian government services and office building, the Egyptian museum, that housed the largest collection of Egyptian antiquities in the world, and numerous commercial and residential buildings. Logos of Western fast-food franchises stood next to local shops that had their goods often sprayed onto the pavement. Tahrir Square was a primary hub for the city, a central thoroughfare to get to different parts of the city. The square was a place to get stuck in traffic and a place where foreign tourists were shaken together with Egyptians.

While studying abroad, my classes were strewn across the three campuses and the serenity and familiarity of a college campus was interrupted by the cacophony of the city as I walked from class to class.

The first time I saw a group of young children, without adult supervision, and shoeless begging students for money as they walked from campus to campus, I felt equal parts uncomfortable, sad, and confused.

Where were their parents or caretaker? Why were they not in school in the middle of the day? Did they live nearby? Why wasn't anyone watching them?

Naively, this was my first time experiencing this type of poverty that exists in so much of the world. This level of poverty allows kids to roam around without anyone batting an eye. This level of poverty makes statistics about people living on less than one dollar a day in tear-jerking donation ads.

One time, I asked a fellow Egyptian classmate about the kids that hung around the campus and why they weren't in school. They shrugged and simply said, "they're street kids," as if that should explain it.

At the time, I couldn't tell whether I was more jarred by the kids or by the lack of reaction by the students walking by them without a second glance. Clearly, seeing these kids was part of the tapestry of the city, as routine as the five times daily call to prayer or the pollution that blanketed the city.

I kept change on hand to give to basically anyone who asked for it. Sometimes I'd give away snacks or food I had with me. I The absolute least I could do felt so inconsequential to practically be meaningless. These kids clearly needed much more than an Egyptian pound or a box of juice to have any chance of changing their circumstances.

This kind of poverty was devoid of hope.

I had been raised on the promise of lifting oneself up by their bootstraps. The ability to change ones' circumstance through hard work and sacrifice was the promise of the "American dream."

What happens when you don't have bootstraps — or even shoes?

* * *

I worked at an international development organization whose goal was to provide economic opportunity for kids like the ones who frequented the AUC campus. My work had the potential to have far greater impact than the Egyptian pounds I distributed during my study abroad days. When my workplace organized a donation drive in coordination with a local Egyptian non-profit, I volunteered to help lead the charge. The non-profit raised money to purchase and give pregnant cows to women, usually single mothers, who lived in Egyptian villages. The idea was to help these women earn a longer-term income stream.

Several months after the end of the donation drive, the non-profit asked for another colleague and I to visit the women who received pregnant cows through our charitable contributions. They wanted to share the success stories of the women so office staff could understand the direct impact to inspire future donations.

The village where the women lived was a two-to-three-hour drive outside of Cairo in the Nile Delta. The Delta, named because of its triangular shape, absorbs the traveling silt that originates downstream in Ethiopia before making its way north and disembarking in the stretch of land between Cairo and the Mediterranean Sea. ancient and modern Egyptians alike relied on the Delta for its rich agricultural land to produce a myriad of foodstuffs and other goods, perhaps most famously producing papyrus and cotton ("Nile River", 2022). Cairo, Alexandria, Damietta, Rosetta (or *Rachid* in Arabic) in addition to numerous other cities, well-known to Egyptians but less familiar to foreigners, pepper the Nile Delta as an estimated 50% or more of the population call the Nile Delta home (Fishar, 2018). It is theorized Herodotus referred to the Nile Delta when claiming that, "Egypt is the gift of the Nile" (Griffiths, 1966).

I could be forgiven for expecting a place of such natural wealth would translate into individual wealth.

The site of our shiny, white van driving into the village caused quite a stir. When I walked out of the van, a white woman, I quickly became an attraction to the villagers unused to seeing foreigners. News of our visit quickly spread in the small village and, for the remainder of the day, a herd of children followed us around, clearly thinking a white foreigner was reason to pause whatever else they would have been doing with their day.

Our group included a fellow Egyptian colleague, a representative from the non-profit, and the driver who had taken us to the village. The non-profit representative was very eager to introduce us to each of the four women and for us to hear their stories.

We met each woman at their home. Two lived in the center of the village while the other two lived on the outskirts and required us to drive further to get there.

The first woman we met eagerly showed us the cow, which lived with her in her house. The house had a dirt floor with no running water and a roof made of a variety of metals. The woman and her children shared a non-enclosed space to sleep, and the cow lived across the hall in a makeshift stall.

She explained she had sold the calf to pay for a surgery that her child desperately needed. She also proudly told us that the cow was pregnant again with another calf, and they sold the milk to cover the expenses of the animal and made a little extra money.

The next woman had sold both the cow and calf, she explained apologetically. She said her husband who had passed away recently left a number of debts she needed to pay. She used the remainder of the money to pay for new clothes for her children.

The third woman, arguably, had the most success from the donation. She lived just outside the village with her daughters and niece. When we arrived, all four of them were sitting around an open oven making bread.

They not only had the cow and calf, but the cow had since had another calf. They turned the milk into butter and cheese, which they sold in the village. The profits from the butter and cheese sales allowed them to purchase the bread oven, further enhancing the business.

This woman seemed to have a knack for business as she explained her plans to purchase other livestock to complement the dairy business. She seemed very proud of employing the other women in her household and being able to give them a sustainable income.

The last woman, however, has stuck with me the most. Her story best paints the picture of what happens when someone has no options, no help, and no hope.

She lived with her almost adult son. She didn't know exactly his diagnosis as she didn't have the money to go to Cairo to access the right doctors, but he was severely mentally impaired and non-verbal, and he had been since he was born, she explained.

She said her husband had left her when her son was only a small child. She said he didn't know how to deal with the boy or want to stick around to support them. She had cared for him alone for almost two decades. Most of their food came from the small plot of land they lived on, and any income come from an odd job in the village cleaning or sewing. For the most part, they were self-sufficient in terms of their most basic needs. While we had driven from the village to where she lived, she had no such luxury and would walk the several miles into the village when needed.

She brought us to her one-room house where they both lived. The cow stood nearby on a leash. My colleague asked her how the cow changed her life.

"My son and I only eat what we can grow. Now we can drink milk. Sometimes we trade the milk for chicken or meat," she explained.

"And where do you keep the cow?" asked the man from the non-profit.

"He stays right outside the house, where he is now. During the day my neighbor lets him wander into their land to eat," she said very matter of fact.

"I can barely take care of myself and my son, much less the cow," she went on.

"Is there anything else you hope to do with the cow?" my colleague asked.

"I hope to save enough money to take my son to the city to see a doctor who can tell me how to help him," she said.

Years later, that day spent meeting these four women remains vivid. I knew the statistics that roughly 25-30% of Egyptians lived below the national poverty line at the time but witnessing and hearing these women's stories made the impact real (CAPMAS, 2010). These women were all doing the best they could with everything they had available, and not one of them had consistent and reliable electricity and running water. They graciously accepted the charity of a pregnant cow but needed much more than a cow to change the trajectory in their or their children's economic future.

Egypt's national narrative seemed to not exist here.

What kind of national narrative can exist when becoming a parent or an accident or an unplanned circumstance can immediately alter one's economic opportunity for the rest of their life? What does it mean if one's earning potential, education, and career is practically set from the moment of birth?

These four women felt like a parable with no actionable lesson other than, "don't be born poor."

I wonder often about these women, particularly the last two. What could the enterprising woman who had turned her cow into a small business employing her female relatives have become if she had, for instance, been able to access higher education — or any education. Maybe she could have obtained a business degree and started a disruptive start-up or become an executive at a company. Maybe she would have invented a new product or service that employed thousands.

What if the woman with the handicapped son had been able to get him treated by a doctor? Maybe her son could have accessed therapy or treatment so he could learn to live independently or hold a job. Maybe she could have had her own steady job.

These kinds of long-term systemic support structures are difficult to raise money for through a one-off charity event.

Egyptians plugged holes. Through mosques or churches or through family networks, people looked after one another to provide these support structures as best they could.

Without strong, equitable, and basic government service provisions, the holes are too big to plug though. Too many people are left stranded by life and are unable to do anything other than tread water. All that potential and individual contribution is left unnourished.

Economic uncertainty can make it impossible to focus on anything beyond the immediate set of needs, which makes it easier for political interests to ignore the underlying issues. Too many people living without enough hope is like parts of a tree turning into kindling and waiting for the right spark to set ablaze.

People are averse to change until the moment they feel the need to change as if it was a basic necessity. When they get to that point, anything is possible.

CHAPTER 8:

A DIFFERENT PANDEMIC

Before we go further, I want to take a quick commercial break to give a heads up that the next section will discuss sexual harassment and assault.

I want to tell my story, however, I first want to explain and educate the context to amplify and name the incredible Egyptian women change agents and to dispel myths. I write this very aware and wary of co-opting Egyptian women's stories because they need no help from me in using their voices.

Perceptions and stereotypes abound in Western society about Muslim and Middle Eastern women. These views feel completely at odds with my experience, and I hope to shed light on the reality and to help cut away at preconceived notions.

Women have agency, they have passion, and they have courage. Those, I believe, are shared traits around the world.

Back to our regularly scheduled programming.

* * *

Egyptians faced many challenges in the years I lived in Egypt. Egyptian women also contended and continue to contend with constant sexual harassment.

A national dialogue about the pandemic of street harassment gained steam around the time I moved to Cairo.

In 2006, a case of mass sexual assault on women took place during the Muslim holy holiday of Eid el Fitr, which marks the end of Ramadan. Women in downtown Cairo were attacked by a group of men who groped them, tore off their clothes, and assaulted them (Al Bawaba, 2012). One of my study abroad friends had been in downtown Cairo during that time and described the panic and fear of suddenly having a frenzy of men attacking women all at once. She only narrowly escaped more direct assault because a shopkeeper marshalled as many women inside his cramped shop as possible and closed the metal security gate.

The Egyptian Center for Women's Rights (ECWR) in 2008 found that 83% of Egyptian women and 95%+ foreign women reported being sexually harassed based on their report "Clouds in Egypt's Sky" that spoke with more than 2000 Egyptian men and women across the country. The report goes on to compare beliefs about who likely gets harassed to the realities of what women reported experiencing. Specifically, they found that while many believe women who dress more modestly or cover their hair or face immunize themselves from harassment, the findings show that women regardless of the way they dress experience harassment. In 2013, another study conducted by UN Women called "Study on Ways and Methods to Eliminate Sexual Harassment in Egypt" found that 99.3% of Egyptian women surveyed across Egypt reported experiencing sexual harassment, with the most frequent locations of this harassment being the street and public transportation.

Unfortunately, numbers don't take action or compel people to change. Stories do.

In October 2008, Egypt convicted and sentenced someone for the first time for sexual harassment or assault after the women who was attacked dragged her attacker to the police. That woman, 27-year-old filmmaker Noha Rushdi or Noha Ostadh, dragged the man Sheriff Gomaa to the police station after he grabbed her breasts repeatedly from the van he was driving which caused her to fall to the ground. Somehow, she wrestled him from his vehicle and, reportedly, had to convince the police to take her accusations seriously (BBC, 2008).

When I first moved to Egypt, the case was being widely reported in both the Egyptian and international media. The reporting of this case opened the door to a wider recognition of what Egyptian and foreign women already knew — walking as a woman in Cairo could be, at best, uncomfortable and, at worst, dangerous.

While Noha bravely brought her attacker to justice, she was not alone in advocating for change.

Groups like ECWR, author of the 2008 sexual harassment study, launched a public awareness campaign. El Nadeem Centre for the Management and Rehabilitation of Victims of Violence, Nazra for Feminist Studies, and New Women Foundation were all examples of Egyptian non-governmental organizations (NGO) working to promote women's rights, which included addressing street harassment. In 2008, New Women Foundation coordinated more than twenty groups to form the Task Force for Combating Sexual Violence that drafted language to amend the Egyptian penal code to criminalize sexual harassment according to a 2014 report called "Egypt: Keeping Women Out," co-authored by a number of Egyptian women's rights organizations.

In 2010, an Egyptian movie came out called "678," a reference to the bus one of the main characters took to get to work and the setting of her daily brushes with men trying to grope her. The film used multiple storylines (one of which was based on Noha Rushdi's experience) to describe different types of gender-based violence Egyptian women experienced and call attention to their psychological impacts.

The movie in Egypt was revolutionary for weaving together the everydayness of what Egyptian women experienced. It also demonstrated how sexual harassment and the cycle of shame, anger, and fear could cross socioeconomic boundaries even in a country where those boundaries acted as fortified borderlines. The movie depicts the stares, comments, and "accidental" touches women in Egypt experience regularly — and how these experiences can galvanize women into action.

HarassMap, founded in 2010 around the same time as the release of the movie "678," sought to mobilize everyday women to fight sexual harassment on the ground by creating a platform for women to report incidents of sexual violence to create a heat map of the city. Their website states, "In this environment, it was our opinion that advocacy for a new law on sexual harassment could not stand alone in a context in which existing laws are not enforced because sexual harassment is not seen as a crime, or even as something wrong. So, we decided to tackle what we believe is the source of non-enforcement — social acceptability."

Their map, which myself and many of my friends used and contributed to with our own experiences, helped create data where it did not exist to help showcase the breadth and depth of the problem in real time.

Egyptian women also got creative.

The Bussy Project, a play on the word "pussy" in English that in Arabic means "look" or "see," used performance art to allow women to share their stories across the full spectrum of violence against women by holding storytelling workshops and performances.

Egyptian women also fought the disease of sexual harassment by learning to fight by taking karate classes to learn defensive techniques (Fraser, 2009) and creating the Tahrir Bodyguards which, founded by Soraya Bahgat following the 2011 revolution, was a group that would defend female protesters from attack.

Building on the experience of HarassMap, Egyptian women more recently have created new social media channels and accounts to aggregate their experiences. Not satisfied with only reporting that an incident took place, Instagram accounts like @assualtpolice aim to name perpetrators to get police attention; the handle has over 340,000 followers as of June 2022 (note the syntax of the handle in English would probably be "Assault, Police!" as the intention of the posts is to get justice for survivors). @assualtpolice was founded by Nadeen Ashraf, who began the account to specifically document cases against a particular male student at the American University in Cairo who had a history of sexually harassing women. He was eventually arrested and convicted after numerous other survivors came forward anonymously. Other sites like the blog *al-Modowana* and the Instagram account @Speak Up, similarly provide Egyptian women with a space to document and name those that harass or assault them anonymously, which was important in a country that sometimes targets women who accuse men, according to Sara Tonsy in an article about "Mobilization by and for women."

These women built on a long history of women's rights activism.

Arguably the most well-known Egyptian female leader to most Americans is Cleopatra, although she is far from the only example. Less well known but equally as crafty, Shagarat al-Durr ruled Egypt briefly in the thirteenth century. Born into slavery, she became a concubine and then wife of sultan Salih Ayyub, the last sultan of the Ayyubid era. Al-Durr became the de facto ruler during her husband's long military absences, and when he died, she concealed his passing to allow her time to take control with support from Mamluk (an enslaved military class that fought the Crusaders and, eventually, ruled Egypt). She even bested Ayyub's son. Although she remarried, which technically meant handing over the reins of power to her new husband, she is widely regarded as having control over the key decisions until her assassination several years later (Levanoni, 2022).

Numerous examples from Egypt's more recent history also demonstrate women's long-time crusade to have agency in their lives and to fight for change. Huda Sha'arawi, born in 1879 into the *harem* system that separated men and women, famously threw off her veil covering her hair in public in 1923 during a time this was outlawed. She sought to encourage other women to do the same to protest the exclusion of women's rights and bring it into the national dialogue following Egypt's liberation from British colonialism. She eventually fought to raise the marriage age to sixteen (she was married when she was thirteen to her cousin who was forty years her senior) and founded the Egyptian Feminist Union in 1923 (Rachidi, 2019).

Following in Sha'arawi's footsteps, Nawal El Saadawi, born in 1931, was a doctor, writer, and activist who rose to prominence in the early 1970s with the publishing of her book, *Women and Sex*. The book sought to end the practice of female genital mutilation (commonly referred to as FGM), which was a common practice in Egypt even though not grounded in Islam. She detailed her personal experience with the procedure, which was forced upon her at the age of six. FGM was eventually outlawed in Egypt in 2008 due in part to El Saadawi's activism and spotlight on the issue. El Saadawi advocated for many changes for Egyptian women, often her positions faced stiff opposition and at one point earned her a stint in prison (Ali, 2021; Cowell, 2021).

Egyptian women had many role models for fighting both the broader systems of repressive government and the inequality they experienced in their country. I often think the reason the Middle East has some of the most repressive laws in the world against women is because the men who rule those countries simply fear the strength of their women citizens.

Like many efforts to create change, these brave women also faced backlash.

I heard numerous stories from my Egyptian female friends about their experiences getting sexually harassed or assaulted. Sometimes, if not often, my Egyptian friends talked about these incidents like they were recounting what they did over the weekend. One time an Egyptian female friend who covered her head with a hijab, recounted being followed and groped by a man when exiting a metro station. Her reflection at the end of the story? *A'ady, ya'any* (normal).

Other female friends, who had the luxury of hiring private drivers to ferry them around Cairo, were aghast at the idea of taking a common taxi much less riding the metro or taking a bus because of the likelihood of getting groped.

A 2010 survey of young people in Egypt conducted by the Population Council found that almost 80% of men and 73% of women under the age of thirty felt that a woman deserved to be harassed if she dressed provocatively. The 2008 report "Clouds in Egypt's Sky" found that many believed women who did not cover their hair with a hijab or wore short skirts were more likely to be harassed (although their findings disproved this).

They also found that only a miniscule percentage of Egyptian women (2.4%) reported sexual harassment cases to the police. Some examples of Egyptian women's experiences make it easy to understand why.

One woman who was groped by a man on a motorcycle said she was encouraged by onlookers to let the man go and not press charges. She eventually pressed charges but expressed concern about whether that would impact her ability to get married (Birnbaum, 2012). Activist Soraya Bahgat describes women not only being blamed for causing their own harassment but being actively turned away by police from even filing a report (Bremner, 2020). In 2018, a woman posted a video of a man repeatedly trying to ask her out after she claims he had stalked her from a bus station. Debates raged online and in the media about whether or not she was over-reacting (Al Jazeera, 2018).

Not only were women discouraged from making reports but, like in the case of Egyptian-American writer Mona Eltahawy who described her account first-hand in The Guardian in 2011, sometimes assaulted by the police themselves. In another case, a seventeen-year-old Egyptian girl described her rape on a video she posted to social media. According to Vogue Middle East, the girl was "arrested and accused of 'inciting debauchery and violating family values.'"

The Egyptian government had a bifurcated response to the pushes made by Egyptian women activists to combat sexual harassment. On the one hand, Egypt amended the Egyptian Penal Code to "define and criminalize sexual harassment... in August 2021 it was amended to turn sexual harassment from a misdemeanor into a felony and increase penalties for it." Policy change felt like a win, an acknowledgement of the problem, and a directional change in addressing pervasive sexual harassment and assault. On the other hand, numerous female protesters reported being subjected to "virginity tests" by the Egyptian military during the Egyptian revolution. One woman, Samira Ibrahim, brought a case against one of the military doctors she claimed conducted a "virginity test" against her will after stripping her of her clothes and beating her. The case got attention after she released a video about her experience that went viral. The doctor was eventually acquitted of all charges and the military denied this occurred (Rageh, 2012). Nevertheless, a decade later an Egyptian military general admitted "virginity tests" were used in leaked audio (Middle East Monitor, 2020).

The backlash makes Egyptian women's activism and willingness to publicly tell their stories even more incredible; we can learn so much from them.

In July 2011, the *New York Times* ran a story titled "Women in Egypt Face Serious Harassment Every Day," describing the situations and numerous efforts by Egyptian women to combat harassment. In October 2020, The *New York Times* ran a story called "The 22-Year-Old Force Behind Egypt's Growing #MeToo Movement," about Nadeen Ashraf's founding of the @ assualtpolice Instagram account. The title of the article makes it seem as if Egyptian women picked up the fight as part of an American-initiated movement against sexual harassment and assault, when in reality the most recent examples like Ashraf were part of a generations-long inoculation campaign against sexual harassment led by Egyptian women — their stories were the early antibodies.

Inspired by my Egyptian sisters, I'll tell you my story too.

CHAPTER 9:

A DIFFICULT STORY

———

At times, I had a love/hate relationship with Egypt — the "hate" was caused by the daily, routine sexual harassment that I faced when I dared to walk on the street or exist in public.

Sexual harassment and assault were not new to me as they are not uniquely Egyptian problems.

Growing up, I pieced together conversations my parents didn't intend for me to hear about my mom having male colleagues grab her or make inappropriate comments.

I even vividly remember the first time a group of high school boys catcalled me from their pickup truck window while I was running. I was fifteen and had never thought twice about my clothes when running in the sticky Florida heat, but that one incident robbed me of my peace of mind and made me wary about running alone while wearing shorts and a tank top; I couldn't help but wonder if I had caused the suggestive and lewd comments. Another time, working my first job in a restaurant, a man made a crude joke about my backside as I walked away from the table, and the other men sitting with him laughed uproariously.

Going to school in New York City, I learned week one the defensive trick of walking with my keys through my fingers when walking alone and with my university-provided and -branded rape whistle close by, just in case. Sexual harassment towards women and girls was so pervasive it took a hashtag to get people to pay attention. Even that, however, did not prepare me for what I experienced in Egypt. I came to expect that I would be sexually harassed in some way every time I walked outside my apartment door. Every. Single. Time. A man followed me home from campus on his bike, getting almost close enough to touch me and plenty close enough for me to hear him tell me what he wanted to do to me. I received harassment from the obvious stares by men as I passed them on the street and the suggestive comments, under their breath or right to my face, often in Arabic that they assumed I didn't understand, but I increasingly did. Sometimes I would ask Mohamed what a word meant that I heard a man say. He would turn red and refuse to give me the translation.

On many occasions, a man would "accidentally" bump into me in the corner store or brush up against me as I was grabbing a bottle of water from the drink fridge, even though there was plenty of space for him to have avoided touching me.

Often, a taxi driver who would reposition the multiple extra stuck-on mirrors in my direction and shoot frequent glances at me sitting in the backseat. Sometimes one of his hands might go missing from the steering wheel.

Sometimes, I would engage in conversations, usually with taxi drivers, that I at first eagerly started to practice my Egyptian Arabic but quickly learned to avoid because they often turned from a comment about the traffic to pointed, personal questions about my marital status. The answer to "are you married" if you are a woman in Egypt, I learned quickly, was always yes; I always wore a fake wedding band as did most of my foreign female friends — not that it worked.

I developed an aversion to sitting in the passenger seat of a taxi that followed me for a long time back to the US , after experiencing several incidents when the driver took that to mean something it did not..

Occasionally, expensive cars near fancy hotels that would slow down, roll down a window, and proposition me in broad daylight, expecting me to accept the offer.

The frequent phone harassment meant getting repeated calls by men who somehow found our phone numbers (my friends and I theorized whoever sold us the phones took note of our numbers) and would call incessantly. Sometimes they said nothing but merely breathed heavily on the other end. I saved them in my phone as "Harasser 1" or "Harasser 37." Given that few people had unlimited monthly phone plans and instead paid by the minute, I would sometimes pick up the phone and set it down where I couldn't hear to run through the man's minutes without actually talking to him.

One time, a man who exposed himself to my roommate when she was alone in the elevator with him on the way to our tenth-floor apartment.

After a flare-up of violence at a football match between Egypt and Algeria, a Central Security Force officer refused to let me by without groping me.

While passing me on his bike, a man tried to grope me as I walked home.

A man spit on me because I dared to turn around and call him out for following my friends and I for multiple city blocks in downtown Cairo.

It felt relentless.

It all had the same chilling effect: I was on edge and anxious. I came to expect the harassment. I didn't know how or when, but I knew throughout the course of my day to expect it. Every time I left my apartment, I felt like I turned into someone else; it wasn't Catherine walking around the streets of Cairo but a stone-faced statue that could flip between ignoring the constant advances to reacting quickly to call attention to a man that felt threatening.

Similar to going to school in New York City, I soon learned a handful of survival tactics to get through the day. I had headphones and listened to music to block out most of the comments, sunglasses so men wouldn't think or couldn't tell if I was making eye contact, a long coat that went to my knees (if bearable given the temperature), and a cell phone to pretend to make a phone call in a taxi to fend off an unwanted conversation.

I tried to become invisible in order to be left alone.

Sometimes I wouldn't want to leave the apartment all day because the thought of dealing with the combination of Cairo's chaos and the constant harassment felt intolerable. Harassment was so common that it went right after the weather in our nightly roommate debriefs about the day.

"Man, the pollution levels were off the charts today! I feel like I'm breathing out black dust."

"Agree! And guess what happened in the [taxi or on the street or while buying a bottle of water or in the elevator] today..."

I went through cycles of how I responded to these incidents. Sometimes I used my superpower to ignore even someone practically whispering in my ear as I walked down the street. Other times, I needed to say something to every person who so much as glanced in my direction. Eventually, exhausted from the effort, I would revert back to being invisible and silent. The cycle would begin again.

Even when I wanted to, I often didn't respond quickly enough or lost my words, particularly in Arabic. I replayed missed moments and lost chances, kicking myself over and over for not saying something at all or not saying the "right" thing, as if there could be a right thing to say.

I was victimized twice. Once by the harasser and a second time by myself.

I was weighed down by my inability to change this behavior. Surely, if I confronted enough men in Cairo eventually that would make a dent? Not only did these men steal my safety but my agency to make change.

Sometimes the confrontations were cathartic since they felt like the only way to fight back or stand up for myself. But mostly they felt exhausting and humiliating. My individual attempts at something akin to justice felt practically pointless. Even if the right laws were on the books, which they technically were, how would I both apprehend the man and prove it?

Luckily, an incident happened where all the right ingredients came together to allow me to pursue justice.

I was going to the wedding of a Christian colleague with several other friends and colleagues. I hadn't gone to many Egyptian weddings or formal affairs so I hesitated as I put on a sleeveless dress, the only dress I had that was formal enough for a wedding.

Although Egypt does not legally regulate what women can and cannot wear, I had quickly updated my wardrobe to include almost exclusively loose fitting and non-revealing clothing; like my long trench coat, it was a safety blanket taking away a justification for getting harassed.

I put on my black dress and a shawl around my shoulders. What could possibly happen while at a wedding?

I still felt uncomfortable going out of my house with shoulders and legs uncovered as I waited for a couple colleagues to pick me up. I felt like I was asking for it.

In Coptic Christian weddings guests gather outside the doors of the church to watch as the bride arrives with her family to celebrate her as she walks in. My colleague, the bride, got out of the car, and we all cheered and shouted. In that moment, I forgot any of my anxieties about what I was wearing and felt safe in the crowd of familiar people.

That feeling did not last long — as we all turned to follow the bride into the church, I felt a hand grab my buttocks, hard

I turned my head to catch the man's eye as he walked away, a haughty smirk appearing on his face, like he was mocking me and believed he got away with it.

After years of getting harassed and hours spent agonizing over missing an opportunity, my instincts kicked in and I knew what to do.

I yelled and ran after him in my heels.

He got several feet away before I grabbed onto his plaid button-down shirt and yelled not "harasser" but "thief," a trick I learned to get much more attention. Calling him a thief wasn't even inaccurate since this man and others like him are thieves — they steal agency, safety, and the ability to simply exist without a threat of harm.

Realizing what happened, several of my colleagues heard me and rushed over.

While I tried to quickly communicate what happened and that I wanted to bring him to the nearest police station, he broke away from my grip. The fact I had managed to hang on to him that long said everything about the amount of adrenaline pumping through me.

One of my friends ran after him and tackled him to the ground a block away.

Eventually we were able to drag him to the police station that was, thankfully, not too far away from the church.

I sat in a dingy, dimly lit Egyptian police station with an officer behind the desk looking skeptically at me and probably wondering why I was sitting in front him.

Egyptians typically try to steer clear of Egyptian police at all costs; they are well-known for corruption and intense brutality against political dissidents and ordinary citizens alike. Citizens, particularly poorer citizens, were frequently harassed for money by police trying to prove to the general population that the government existed. This included fining a shopkeeper for setting prices too high or suddenly enforcing a minor traffic law that no one followed by pulling over a taxi driver and demanding money lest they be jailed or worse. This type of frequent, random, and ad hoc justice system meant Egyptians would avoid interactions with the police if they could help it.

Egyptians who got caught up in these police schemes and questioned the police's authority with even the most basic questions about why they were being targeted could be subject to brutal treatment or harassment. In an article about the police post-Egyptian revolution, Salwa Ismail describes how police often employed disrespect or humiliation as a tactic to wield their authority, for example by calling an older man "boy" or insulting them publicly.

In one of the most famous cases of police brutality, a young twenty-eight-year-old entrepreneur living in Alexandria named Khaled Said was approached by police while sitting in an Internet café. Most believed he was of interest by the police because he had filmed a scene of police "sharing the spoils of a drug bust" on his personal blog. Reports suggest that officers asked for money and when Said refused, the police began beating him in the café and then dragged him outside to the street where they continued the assault. He died on the scene (Ahram Online, 2012).

Pictures of his beaten face circulated online and one activist, later revealed to be an Egyptian Google employee named Wael Ghonim, started a Facebook group called "We are all Khaled Said" that quickly attracted tens of thousands of followers across Egypt.

While numerous efforts existed to protest treatment of Egyptians by police, Said's death seemed to hit a nerve because he did not seem to be a threat, despite the government's attempt to accuse him of drug possession after his death and came from a solidly middle class background.

As one commentator put it to the Daily Beast, "His death made the connection between the advocacy and the everyday life of Egyptians. It made the point that everyone can be affected."

I knew all this as a I sat in the police station hoping for justice against this man who stole my right to not be violated on the street. I either naively or quite accurately believed my whiteness and my American passport would shield me from the kinds of treatment most Egyptians could expect from the Egyptian police. I also knew about women like Noha Rushdi. Telling my story was the least I could do.

On the way to the police station, I had called Mohamed, in tears, to tell him what happened.

"Are you okay? Where are you now?" Mohamed asked after I told him in fragmented sentences what happened.

"I'm okay, I'm with Amr, from work," I said.

"Okay, I'm on the other side of the city. I'll try to get to you, but it might take more than an hour. Let me call Ahmed and see if he can come by, he doesn't live far away," Mohamed said.

Our friend Ahmed arrived shortly afterwards, which made me feel better. Yet, sitting there I felt fear, shame, and an unrelenting wave of anger.

Although I knew I had done nothing wrong, I still felt responsible for what happened because I was sitting there in this dress that I wouldn't have worn anywhere else in Cairo, and I knew that I would be asking for trouble the minute I put it on. Why had I not just worn a loose, flowy less formal work dress? Couldn't I have at least kept my knee length coat on until we got into the church? Why had I thought being in a crowd of people I knew would keep me safe?

The police officer asked me to explain what happened. I recounted what happened in a mixture of my own Arabic and help from Ahmed who translated for the officer to record.

As we were talking, I felt from the way the officer looked at me that he was judging me for what I was wearing and judging me for having played a part in the whole incident by daring to wear a dress in public.

The worst part about it was that I felt the same way in that moment.

We got the through story, and the police officer informed me that the next day I needed to go to the local courthouse to explain my story to one of the local judges or clerks so that they could officially process charges against the man.

The next day, I trekked across the city again to the court-house near the incident and recounted my story with the harasser sitting on a chair behind me to a skeptical lawyer clearly having similar thoughts to the police officer the night before.

I recounted my story in my only half-decent Egyptian Arabic since the attorney led me to believe he did not speak English. The attorney asked me some standard questions.

"What did this man do?"

"He grabbed my butt." I demonstrated this point with a pencil holder the man had on his desk.

"Are you sure this is the right person?"

"Yes, I am 100% sure."

And then, "What were you wearing?"

I paused. "Why do you want to know?"

The attorney then says, in English, "This man is studying to be a lawyer. He's engaged to be married. Do you understand that this could ruin his life if you press charges?"

I realized this man was not on my side and he was probably going to make my life very difficult. Nonetheless I looked him in the eyes and I said, "I understand, but I'm not the one that did something wrong."

The attorney made sure he had all my contact information, including my passport number that I, like any expat, had memorized and said he would be in touch.

It would be nice to say that this had a happy ending where my pursuit of justice worked out and that all those other previous incidents had led to this moment where I could finally feel like I made a dent or even one small change.

Instead, the next day I started getting calls from a number that I didn't recognize on my phone. I typically didn't pick up unknown numbers given the amount of phone harassment but because I knew I might get a call from the government lawyer I spoke to the previous day, I answered.

I picked up the phone, and it was a woman on the other line, which felt like it could be important. The woman didn't speak great English, so I got a colleague to take the phone call to translate.

"What did she say? Who is she?" I asked my colleague as she simultaneously had the phone to her ear and was listening to the audibly upset woman.

"She said she's the fiancé of the man you accused of harassing you the other day. She wants you to drop the charges," she said and then turned her attention back to the phone.

"She says her family can offer you money if you do. She's saying it will ruin his life and hers," she continued.

I could hear the woman on the other end of the phone grow more upset.

"What is she saying?" I asked.

"She's saying that he is a good man, that he didn't mean to do anything wrong, and that he will never do it again," she said. "What do you want me to say?"

I quickly debated with myself inside my head.

This is partially your fault for wearing a dress, and what about his innocent fiancé? Would this mean her life could be ruined too? Plus, it's not like you're physically injured or like he raped you, I thought to myself.

Yeah, but what about all the times you or your friends have been grabbed or groped or worse and haven't been able to do anything. How can you let this chance go? I continued in my head.

Out loud I said, "Tell her I'm not dropping the charges. And how in the world did she get my number?"

After some rapid Arabic, my colleague replied, "The police gave it to her."

Given that the police may also have given her and her fiancé's family my home address, I moved out of my apartment for about a week and stayed with a friend. The doorman of my building was brought into the loop about what was going on, and he kept an eye on whether anyone stopped by.

Mohamed also called the number back and told them that they were not to call me again. Of course, they did call back numerous times although I never picked up. Eventually, they stopped calling, and I returned to my apartment; I did not renew my lease when it was up a couple months later and, instead, found a new apartment nearby.

I never found out what happened to him. Not long after the Egyptian revolution broke out and police stations became a target of protester frustration, and many were ransacked or set on fire. The courts had bigger problems post-revolution than my small sexual harassment charge.

At the time, I clung to the idea that this would not have happened in America or if it had, something more would have been done. I built up this idea of things that would or wouldn't happen back home to cope with the daily barrage of street harassment.

That untruth was my life raft, along with the rationalizations about how what was happening was not that bad; it was not until reading Roxane Gay's "Not That Bad" collection of essays that I realized I was allowed to believe that my experience was as bad as it felt. It took me longer to realize that violence towards women lives on the same scatter plot graph that includes interruptions by male colleagues to an inability to make healthcare choices about one's body to laws restricting women's ability to vote or own property or dress in the way they please to assault and rape.

Women don't need heroes to come and save them, women are already heroes. Women often experience gender-based violence or aggression, get paid less, have fewer role models in positions of leadership and power, overcome greater hurdles to succeed professionally or gain wealth, are responsible for controlling whether they get pregnant, birth children, raise children, take on disproportionate amounts of housework, and are expected to keep a smile on their face. Our superpower is getting through the day.

As in any good superhero movie, there comes a villain so big and so powerful that it takes a team of heroes to fight. Women are often each other's team, but too often they are missing team members. They are going into the game with half their squad.

Men need to continue to be allies and to turn into players on the field instead of bystanders.

Egyptian women have lived with this kind of routine harassment for a long time — much longer than my time living in Egypt. They were the survivors, the heroes, and the change agents.

Their bravery was about to be tested.

CHAPTER 10:

AN IMPORTANT MATCH

Mohamed and I had many talks about the future of our relationship. After two years, I wanted to get serious about applying to graduate school and decided to abandon my longtime goal of law school to get an MBA instead after seeing the impact investment in the private sector could have on job creation and creating economic opportunity.

We discussed at length whether we were ready to get engaged and what it would mean to potentially be long distance if I started school. Ultimately, I agreed to stay longer in Cairo to give myself time to take graduate exams and to move forward in our relationship. We talked generally about getting married.

On a trip to India together, we visited the Taj Mahal and got there at sunrise to see the unique way the light hits the marble that early in the morning.

When we arrived, we were close to the only people there. We stopped on the walk towards the main attraction, still a distance away. Mohamed said he wanted to find someone to take a picture of us with the Taj Mahal far enough away in the distance to capture the entire structure.

He found an Australian tourist with a similar model DSLR camera around his neck and asked him to take a picture (despite the small number of visitors, he remained selective on who he would allow to use his camera).

I stood to pose in front of the camera but noticed Mohamed was not moving to stand next to me. I looked in his direction, he looked back at me, and knelt to one knee and took out a ring, a gold intricately carved rose.

"Catherine, will you marry me?" he asked.

We differ on our recollections of my reply. I recall pausing and then excitedly saying "yes!" He says I almost immediately said "yes, yes, yes!"

Thankfully, the Australian tourist had the good sense to continue taking pictures during this entire exchange.

Our lives were about to change in more ways than one.

* * *

One of my favorite Egyptian jokes goes like this:

President Putin comes to Egypt to meet with President Mubarak. Putin asks "President Mubarak, you always win your elections with 95% or more of the vote. Can you help me do the same?"

Mubarak graciously replies, "No problem, I'll send my people to Russia to help you with your next election."

In advance of the next Russian election, Mubarak honors his promise and sends his top campaign advisors to Russia.

Their advice is a success when the Russian election results come back — 95% Mubarak.

Most Egyptians seemed to accept Mubarak's presidency as fact; most of my Egyptian friends, born under Mubarak's rule, believe that he would serve until he died. Mubarak felt everywhere, ever present. His tight grip on the main levers of power in Egypt and his carefully curated visual image made it clear who was in charge. The posters of Mubarak plastered on buildings were a threat to whoever might dare to resist or suggest an alternative.

People closer to the pulse of Egyptian politics already knew by 2010 that this imagery was like a movie set, designed to give the feeling of total control with limited support holding it up.

In August 2010, six months before the revolution "started" *The Daily News Egypt*, an independent English language newspaper in Egypt, ran an interview with Saad Eddin Ibrahim, the founder of the Ibn Khaldun Center for Development Studies, who had recently returned to Egypt. The title of the interview was "Egypt is on the Brink of Revolution." When asked whether a revolution was on the horizon, he replied, "All revolutions are preceded with individual social protests, increasing in numbers and participants. There is a revolution on the horizon, whether it is violent or not depends on the regime, if the government resorted to violence, the people will retaliate."

Many Egyptians did fully support the regime for a variety of reasons.

First, many Egyptians directly benefited from the regime through positions of power in government or the military, jobs within the vast Egyptian bureaucracy, or business gains from direct government contracts or permission to operate. Second, the Egyptian propaganda apparatus was well-funded and effective. The Ministry of Information, and its flagship building in downtown Cairo along the Nile called the Maspero, controlled the Egyptian airwaves and owned many of the larger newspapers and news channels. The Ministry of Information approved which films or television shows were allowed to air and censored foreign films for "morality" and sometimes banned films from airing in Egypt at all; many (most?) Egyptians were aware of this lock on communications and often made the Maspero the site of protests and vandalism. Watching government-run news channels was like watching an alternative set of events or narrative, carefully created to tell a specific kind of truth to the Egyptian public.

Other Egyptians' support for the regime relied merely upon their ability to survive economically. Mubarak had seemingly learned a valuable lesson from the Egyptian bread riots in the 1970s when then President Sadat had tried to lift the subsidies on bread, which created swift anger from the Egyptian public and triggered mass demonstrations and riots across the country. Government-run bread shops with subsidized rates still existed in 2011.

For some, their relationship with the regime was one of "don't ask, don't tell" — don't ask me what I think about the regime, and I won't tell you what I think.

Of course, there were a number of organized opposition groups and activists who pushed for their own space at the table of power like the Muslim Brotherhood or *Kifayah* (enough!), a coalition of opposition forces who came together in 2004 to oppose Mubarak in the runup to the 2005 parliamentary elections.

The Brotherhood, sometimes deemed legal and sometimes banned by the Egyptian government, were as much a political organization as a religious one. Founded in 1928 by Hassan al-Banna, the Brotherhood had formally renounced violence in the 1970s after one of its more famous members Sayed Qutb, whose writings inspired multiple violent groups like al-Qaida and Hamas in calling for an Islamic state, actively called for the violent overthrow of the Egyptian regime (Laub, 2019). Among critics of the Brotherhood, there is active debate about their adherence to that renouncement among all members.

Since the Brotherhood's founding, they dabbled in politics, sometimes running candidates in parliamentary elections and sometimes joining forces with other political groups, even secular, liberal groups, like the Wafd, to achieve similar ends. Their off-again, on-again relationship with political legitimacy often coincided with changes in the Brotherhood's topline leadership vision for the organization and real or perceived openings in the current Egyptian president's tolerance level for general opposition. The Brotherhood moved closer to fully entering the political sphere and pushed for political reforms alongside other oppositions groups and won eighty-eight seats in parliament in 2005; they ran just enough candidates, 161, to get a little less than a third of parliament, seemingly to avoid too directly challenging Mubarak's National Democratic Party (NDP) (Hamzawy and Brown, 2010).

Mubarak delicately balanced the perception of competitive elections and reality. In the 2010 parliamentary elections, the NDP seemed to have a change of heart about its acceptance for political opposition after having passed a law in 2007 drastically reducing judicial oversight from polling locations. Likely fearing increased support for the Brotherhood, the NDP effectively blocked them altogether from the 2010 parliamentary elections. The Wafd, the other main opposition group, boycotted the elections in protest of irregularities. This meant not only that the NDP held 87% of the seats in parliament but, effectively, no true opposition figure could run for president since it was a requirement to hold seats to run (Dunne & Hamzawy, 2010). As Michele Dunne and Amr Hamzawy wrote a little more than a month before the January 2011 revolution began, "the last thing the NDP wants is real opposition competition for the presidency, but the second-to-last thing it wants is the appearance of no competition at all."

The Brotherhood did not just participate in politics. In the 1980s, the group ramped up both the provision of services and their efficient delivery, which was in stark contrast to the way the government operated. They provided subsidized health care to newly minted doctors, discounted textbooks to students, and supported a variety of initiatives aimed at young, less well-off professors. These initiatives were all aimed at a young rising middle-class. These services and advocacy for additional benefits primarily occurred through the Brotherhood's involvement in professional syndicates and student unions under the umbrella of a nation-wide, decentralized organization (al-Awadi, 2009). This organization not only helped the Brotherhood deliver services but created an organizing muscle essentially no other group in Egypt had, the government included, and allowed for community-building and leadership opportunities for the younger generation. In a country with few permitted civil society organizations, the Brotherhood provided a unique opportunity for young people to take on community roles.

At its core, however, the Brotherhood remains an organization that uses religion to inspire, create adherents, and promote a policy agenda. The combination of religion and politics under the umbrella of one organization and one political party creates a potent mix that is primed to quickly activate followers or move the political landscape.

For me, the Brotherhood's presence came across in Egyptian newspaper headlines or in the banners hung around Cairo in the lead up to the 2010 parliamentary elections. The name of the Brotherhood Supreme Guide, Mohamed Badie at the time, was a name I knew like the names of any politician or public figure at home; they simply were part of the national conversation.

Numerous other religiously agnostic, leftist groups also existed, with varying degrees of support and political power. One group called the April 6th movement quickly gained attention. In March 2008, several young Egyptians began a Facebook group in support of a textile workers' strike in the industrial area of El-Mahalla, north of Cairo. Within weeks the group had over 70,000 followers and helped galvanize protests and riots on April 6th, 2008. Several of the leaders, including Esraa Abdel Fattah Rashid and Ahmed Maher, were arrested and questioned. The overnight success of the group launched its leaders, like Maher and Asma Mahfouz, into the spotlight producing headlines even in American news outlets like the 2008 piece in *Wired* called "Cairo Activists Use Facebook to Rattle Regime" and a 2009 piece in the *New York Times* "Revolution, Facebook-style."

While other Egyptian opposition groups like the Wafd, Tagammu, and Arab Nasserist parties existed, and who sometimes formed coalitions with the Muslim Brotherhood to push for reform, they "lack[ed] large constituencies and the ability to build popular support; what little influence they [did] possess c[a]me primarily from the limited-circulation newspapers they publish[ed]" (Shehata, 2008). April 6th brought a new generation of Egyptians into calls for reform and change while spear-heading the usage of social media as a tool for communication, awareness, and mobilization.

These groups and others also used street protests prior to the 2011 revolution to voice dissent or push for change.

Having gone to school in New York City, protests were simply part of the scenery; tree, sidewalk, pigeon, protest.

The first time I went to a protest in Egypt was a little bit different.

Early on after I had moved to Cairo, I had a roommate that was a freelance journalist, or what is called a "stringer" at several international publications. She decided to go and report on a protest against a recent government action - and I decided to tag along. I'd like to note, going to protests in a foreign country simply to bear witness is not something I suggest doing and would not have repeated this excursion in current day. One should either be participating or have a specific purpose, like reporting, to show up, otherwise it distracts from the intention of the protest.

By the time we got to the site of the protest, hundreds had already gathered in a square in downtown Cairo. The signs, written in Arabic, were home-painted on large white cloths, unfurled from neighboring buildings, and held by people on the ground. The crowd was angry, passionate, and loud. They chanted phrases that at the time I did not understand. As with most protests, you don't need to understand the words to understand their meaning.

In many ways, the protest seemed no different from the ones I had seen in New York. Large crowds that were full of passion and anger engaged in repetitive chants to enable individuals to communicate as one. The biggest difference? In downtown Cairo there were hundreds if not thousands of Central Security Forces in riot gear lining the roads and waiting with plastic shields in front of them.

In my naivete, I simply thought they were there to keep the peace.

My roommate and I climbed to the roof of building so we could get a bird's eye view of the square. Then, without warning and at least to us without provocation, the police began moving to disperse the protesters. They marched aggressively towards the group, batons ready and shields in front of their faces.

Again, without warning, someone fired off tear gas.

The noise from the protest shifted from coordinated chants to screams and yelling as pandemonium erupted. Most protesters tried to flee to neighboring side streets while others fought back against police.

The police attacked protesters and dragged some of them away to large black police vans and drove away.

People were running in every direction.

My roommate and I were momentarily shocked at the turn of events.

"What do we do?" she asked.

"I think we need to get out of here, fast," I said.

With that, we ran down many flights of stairs to the street, hearts pounding.

I had no idea what caused the sudden violence, if anything, what the police might do next, or if being a foreign women would immediately attract the wrong kind of attention. We didn't wait to find out. We ran through unfamiliar street after unfamiliar street until we got far enough away to get in a taxi.

I spoke with several Egyptian friends about the event afterwards, conveying my shock at how swiftly and without cause police moved in and the violence they used immediately. Their response?

"*Aa'dy, yaany* (I mean, normal)."

* * *

In addition to political opposition groups, NGOs also actively worked to promote democratic reforms, pushed for change through capacity building, and raised awareness about the importance of freedom of speech. These groups seemed tolerated, largely due to foreign pressure through stipulations in foreign aid (Elmenshawy, 2013).

My expat friends worked in NGOs, journalism, teaching, and a handful worked in diplomatic positions. There were plenty of foreigners working for large corporations, but that tier of expat tended to exist in a parallel and separate universe from my circle of friends They lived in specific compounds in and outside Cairo and often used private drivers to get around the city.

Egypt, and Cairo particularly, often felt to me like organized chaos. I often wondered how the whole city functioned from one day to the next when its city infrastructure was seemingly patched together with tape and Band-Aids. From an informal yet efficient trash collection to a lack of driving rules to the system to get a visa renewed, the city and country operated on an unwritten set of rules and norms about how to survive.

Egypt at the street level often made me feel like rules were something I dreamed up one-night as an absurdist idea. It was easy to forget the underlying bureaucracy that could make getting a legitimate business license next to impossible or that breaking certain rules, like dissent or insults towards the Egyptian regime, could swiftly land you in prison, or worse.

From the numerous conversations I had with Egyptians friends at the time, there were some who felt that the openness to political opposition and the existence of NGOs signaled progress. Other more cynical friends, often closer to activist circles, felt that the Egyptian government would only open the door to freedom of expression and economic progress as wide as foreign governments, particularly the US, made them. They believed the acceptance of civil society organizations and political opposition was likely political theatre to keep the military aid flowing.

My even more cynical friends didn't bother having opinions about the Egyptian regime at all.

At the same time, the economic conditions in Egypt, like much of the Middle East, meant that the uncleared brush of discontent and limited hope for change could as easily turn into a conflagration as it could to crunch under one's feet; people can only be deprived of a voice or of hope for change for so long.

My Egyptian friends and I did not predict what happened next. If I had been paying attention, however, an incident a little more than a year before the start of the Egyptian revolution should have been a clue of how quickly a peaceful, albeit chaotic, city like Cairo could turn on itself overnight.

The clue was a soccer (football) match.

Like many countries outside of the United States, Egyptians take their soccer very seriously. Egypt has a long-running rivalry with fellow North African country Algeria dating back to 1989. In November 2009, Egypt and Algeria were competing against each other for a spot in the 2010 World Cup, when a series of events resulted in a diplomatic spat, protests, and violence (Montague, 2009).

The rivalry between the two countries created an escalation in Egyptian media stoking tensions against the Algerian team. This led a few Egyptian fans to attack the Algerian soccer team's bus. However, rumors then spread that the Algerian team made up the attack.

By the time of the actual match in Cairo, the Egyptian fans were looking for reasons to take their feud off the soccer pitch. Egypt won the game, but because Algeria had won a match in June, it meant the two teams needed to have a third match to determine qualification for the World Cup.

The match happened in Sudan, a neutral country to the Egypt-Algeria rivalry.

Algeria won that final match, sending them to the World Cup. However, Egyptian media reported tens of Egyptian fans were injured by machete-wielding Algerians in Khartoum following the match (FoxSports, 2009). That report was taken as gospel truth by most Egyptians even though it appears that it was an exaggeration, if not an outright falsehood. That reporting, and the loss of a spot at the World Cup, led to massive violence and demonstrations in Cairo.

This was all my Egyptian friends talked about.

"Did you hear what Algeria's fans did to ours?"

"Can you believe the Algerians are trying to cheat their way to the World Cup?"

"I read that they attacked our fans using machetes!"

After the match, Mohamed and I were in my apartment in Zamalek, a neighborhood on an island in the middle of the Nile, watching TV when outside my ground-level living room window we heard shouts and chants. I had never given it a thought before, but I lived almost directly across the street from the Algerian ambassador's residence and several blocks away from the Algerian embassy.

I turned to Mohamed when I heard a noise.

"Do you hear that?" I asked.

"Yeah. Probably someone hit a car and they are arguing about damages."

"Yeah probably," I replied.

A few more minutes passed, and it became clear that the voices we heard outside were not arguing but chanting. The number of voices coming together seemed too many for a common street argument.

I turned to Mohamed and said, "It sounds like they are right outside the window."

He stood up and turned around to look out the window and gasped. Naturally, I stood up to look too.

Standing right below my apartment window, hundreds of incredibly angry Egyptians were chanting and marching. We saw several rocks fly through the air in the direction of the Algerian ambassador's residence. Several people lit a match in front of aerosol cans to create streams of flame in the air.

"Catherine, get away from the window. They might see you and try and throw a brick through," Mohamed said.

My apartment was just off the entrance to the building that would not be difficult for the crowd to enter if they wanted.

We turned on the news to understand what was happening outside or in the rest of the city. The major news outlets had only just begun reporting on the story, and the local ones were spotty in their coverage, perhaps unclear if they were "allowed" by the Ministry of Information to be airing the story. We were able to gather that several protests like the one outside of my window were going on across the city in response to the loss to Algeria.

We didn't know what the crowd would do, if or when the Egyptian police would intervene, or if the crowd would turn their attention on the surrounding buildings. We sat there, cautiously popping our head up to observe what was going on from time to time, but mostly sitting quietly trying not to attract attention.

Eventually, in the late hours of the evening, the crowd began to dissipate, and Mohamed was able to get home.

The next morning, I woke up and left my apartment to a changed neighborhood. One of the main streets in Zamalek had multiple shops vandalized. There were traces of similar protests on the surrounding streets. Pieces of broken debris and rocks littered the streets. I walked from the apartment to the grocery store and encountered rows of Central Security Forces with visible weapons and riot shields that stood in rows across main streets to block access to traffic. Despite the rowdiness of the previous evening, the sheer number of security forces in my neighborhood felt like an overreaction and a dominant show of strength by the government.

The city felt like it had taken a deep breath and was uncertain when to let it out. With few people and fewer cars on the street, Cairo was silent.

While the lost soccer match catalyzed the protests, it felt clear that this intense reaction found its root cause from the more routine pressures and tensions on the population. Poverty, high unemployment, minimal government services, religious tension, little upward mobility, poor education — there were any number of reasons for Egyptians to feel discontent or anxious about their future.

Several of my Egyptian friends debated whether the Egyptian government allowed, if not outright encouraged, the protests as a sort of release valve and distraction from their other grievances. Some felt the protests were a diversion from the main target of many economic and political grievances — mainly, the Egyptian regime. President Mubarak even made a speech about the incident to use the events to provoke national unity. However, over the following weeks this plan backfired as numerous Egyptian newspapers ran columns and stories that redirected anger away from Algeria and towards the Egyptian government for its numerous perceived failings, including the handling of the Egypt-Algeria incident. Many of these headlines focused on Egypt's dignity, summed up best by this quote from an Egyptian living in

Khartoum reported in an article in the *New York Times*, "A Nation's Shaken Ego Seen in a Soccer Loss":

"And if we are really a strong country, why aren't we doing something about it? Nobody had ever insulted the Egyptians to this degree. This issue revealed so many things, it woke up the people."

Despite these events from the several years prior to January 2011, few of my Egyptian friends thought change possible.

Shortly after the Tunisian President Zine El Abidine Ben Ali, or Ben Ali, resigned on January 14, 2011, following massive protests that erupted after fruit seller Mohamed Bouazizi lit himself on fire in frustration over his future economic prospects, I went to lunch with several Egyptian friends.

We were discussing the events in Tunisia and the possibility of similar protests spreading to Egypt.

"Do you think it's possible Egyptians might protest like in Tunisia?" I asked.

"Of course not," said one of my Egyptian colleagues who was fairly well-read about Egyptian democracy movements. "We all know that Mubarak will be the president until he dies — and his father lived to be almost a hundred."

"Plus," another friend said, "we all know his son Gamal is being groomed to be the next President. My children's children will probably live under a Mubarak government."

"Maybe Mubarak will announce some new policy or something to appease activists. But there is no way Mubarak is going anywhere," the first friend said.

Everyone at the table nodded in agreement.

Obviously, we were wrong.

CHAPTER 11:

A VERY LONG DAY

September 11th, January 25th, January 6th.

No one knows a date will become shorthand for a world-changing event when they are brushing their teeth and getting ready for their day.

January 25th, 2011, started like any other day for me in Egypt. I woke up, got ready, hailed a taxi, zoomed through Cairo traffic, gave directions in broken Arabic, dodged cars to cross the six "lane" highway to get to my office, opened my laptop, and started my workday. I had heard about the planned protests but assumed very little would happen given the typical swift response by government security forces to break them up.

Instead, most of my thoughts were on our remaining wedding planning details. Mohamed and I were due to get married in six weeks in my hometown in Florida.

What I did not know, nor did it seem the government, activists had devised a different strategy reportedly borrowed in part from the Serbian Otpor movement that overthrew Slobodan Milosevic (Smithey, 2011). Egyptian activists created a pamphlet that advised protesters to "Assemble with your friends and neighbors in residential streets far away from where the security forces are" and to shout positive slogans while eventually congregating in bigger streets and heading towards government buildings like Parliament (Madrigal, 2011). This strategy would make it far more difficult for security forces to disperse protests because the protesters would come from different places and grow large enough through residential neighborhoods before meeting security forces. Activists in Cairo began protests in multiple neighborhoods, marched and gathered Egyptians as they went, to form several groups of people coming into the Tahrir Square. Similar strategies were taking place across the country.

Throughout the day, security forces attacked protesters, trying to keep them from reaching the main government buildings. In Cairo, many protesters congregated in Tahrir Square after being beaten back from Parliament. Massive numbers of Central Security Forces, run by the Ministry of Interior, were deployed around the city. My typical ride home passed the Maspero, the building where all television and radio communications were controlled. As my taxi passed in front of the buildings, there were huge numbers of security forces lining the building like a moat to keep out invaders.

Surely, Mohamed and I said to each other when we talked that night, there was no way the momentum could be continued. The police brutality served to both punish the protesters and discourage new people from joining. The Egyptian government was too prepared and too well-equipped to let the protests snowball.

The following day a similar set of protests occurred. My colleagues and I all still went to work as if the world had not changed.

The morning of January 26th, I still only had two priorities on my mind: Our wedding and running my first half-marathon in the Upper (southern) Egyptian city of Luxor on January 28th. Outside of work, most of my spare time was divided between late night calls with my mom to pick out wedding invitation fonts or argue over flower arrangements and training for the half marathon with a colleague and friend Helle.

Helle is from Denmark but had lived in Cairo for several years, previously she worked at other development institutions in the Middle East and North Africa. Denmark, she claims, had long been such a homogenous country that people all did their dishes the same way. First, they rinse everything in water, then wash the glasses, then plates, then cutlery, then pots and pans. Then, they wipe the soap and water off with a kitchen towel made of fabric. I would note, they do not rinse off the dishes before drying them. A mystery.

But when she was in middle school, waves of refugees and immigrants, many from the Middle East, began coming into the country. Suddenly, this homogenous country that prided itself on treating everyone equally was tested on extending that principle to these new, foreign people coming into the country.

She says that Danes did not always succeed at doing that. While many of her classmates treated the new students with fear, she, like me, was filled with curiosity that started a journey that ultimately led her to living in Jordan and then Tunisia and then Egypt.

Helle and I were little more than casual colleagues when we started training for the half-marathon but quickly realized we had several things in common. We both immersed ourselves in the local culture and Cairo living, traveled by taxi or metro and not private car like many expats, and traveled extensively around Egypt and the region. We both spoke passable Egyptian Arabic and were well read in Egyptian current events.

We both were endlessly goal-oriented, which meant we followed our half-marathon training plan religiously. We might not pray five times a day, but we did run five times a week.

January 26th was the day before we were due to leave for Luxor to run our half-marathon and it would have taken something momentous to change our plans.

Our office called a meeting that afternoon to discuss the on-going situation and answer any questions we had. Our regional security officer, recently returned from Iraq and Tunisia, assured us that the protests in Egypt would not evolve as quickly as in Tunisia. His belief was the Egyptian security forces were better trained and more equipped.

Most of us, including my Egyptian colleagues, had no reason to disagree.

But, he said, we should all be prepared. He suggested to withdraw cash to have on hand, to make sure to have food and water for a week in our homes in case we couldn't safely make it to a grocery store, to update our phone numbers on the office phone tree, and to print out a copy.

Just in case, he said. Out of an abundance of caution, he said. No need to worry, he said. Highly unlikely there was anything to worry about, he said.

After the meeting, Helle and I approached him to discuss our travel plans.

"Helle and I are planning to fly to Luxor Thursday evening and be back Saturday. Do you think that will be safe?" I asked him.

"Yes, nothing will change in the next couple days, particularly since it's the weekend. If anything, you'll save yourself the hassle from dealing with any road closures from potential protests," he said.

"But, I would make sure to stock up on food and water for when you come back. Just in case," he added.

Like many Muslim-majority countries, the Egyptian weekend is Friday and Saturday to accommodate the *juma'ah* (Friday prayer), which was similar in importance to Sunday church service for Christians. Cairo Fridays typically are a reprieve from the typical traffic and crowds because most people attend Friday prayer at their local mosque and spend time with family; Friday is the day nothing happens.

That evening I scrambled between errands. I went to withdraw cash, go to the grocery store, and pack my weekend bag with the minimal essentials, my running clothes, and two changes of clothes.

Mohamed and I met briefly after work on Thursday to say a quick goodbye. I would only be gone a couple days, so our conversation mostly revolved around logistics.

"I wanted to give you my engagement ring to keep safe while I'm in Luxor. And then you'll pick me up from the airport on Saturday evening?" I asked.

"Yeah, I'll be there," he said. "Call me when you land and get to the hotel. And call me when you finish the race."

"I will. Are you going to the protests on Friday?" I asked.

"I'm not sure. Probably not, they probably won't even be that big," he said.

We said a quick goodbye, the kind of goodbye you say to someone you'll see the next day.

Helle and I set off to the airport together. If I felt nervous, it was only about whether we would hit our goal time for the race. We arrived in Luxor and got to the hostel, where we had splurged on a room with a private bathroom.

One of my favorite places to vacation in Egypt is a place called Ras Shitaan in the Sinai Peninsula that is little more than a camp on a beach. The camps were run by Bedouin, a collection of tribes who had settled in Egypt centuries earlier but kept a distinct culture and heritage from the rest of the population and included huts on the beach where we would sleep on rugs on the floor, use communal bathrooms, and eat communal meals. In comparison, this bare-bones hostel in Luxor felt like luxury.

That morning, Friday January 28th, we woke up and quickly got ready. On the bus ride over to the starting line, we went over for the millionth time our race game plan.

"So we want to be at exactly an hour by kilometer 10," Helle said.

"Yes, or maybe a little under an hour," I replied.

"Catherine, let's not push ourselves too hard in case we need the energy," she said. Helle always plans ahead.

"Good point, let's just see what happens," I said, but secretly still thinking we would push ourselves.

I watched from the bus window as we crossed to the west side of the Nile, home to the Valley of the Kings and Queens where Egyptologists continually discover new tombs. The eastern shore of Luxor, originally the site of the ancient city of Thebes built almost three thousand seven hundred years ago, includes the incredibly preserved Luxor and Karnak Temples.

As we crossed the Nile, the river was so wide you could barely see the other side, and the sun was rising over the Eastern bank, sending rays of light on the ancient sites. I cleared my head of nothing but the plan for the race, giving no thought to the protests or events of the last couple days; they were miles away.

Helle and I ran through the ancient sites of Luxor and for 21 kilometers we rigorously and rigidly hit all the kilometer splits we had planned; I was doubly proud for becoming "fluent" in the metric system. By the end of the race, we were tired, sore, and ecstatic at achieving our goal time. I was exploding with excitement and impatient to call Mohamed and tell him all about the race.

As soon as we got back to our room, I grabbed my phone to call Mohamed. *Ring, ring. Ring, ring.*

"I'm sorry. But the person you are trying to dial is unavailable or has their phone switched off. Please try again later," said the automated, female Vodafone voice.

That's weird, maybe he's still sleeping and turned off his phone before he went to bed? I thought.

I showered, got dressed, and, tried him again. *Ring, ring. Ring, ring.* I got the same automated message.

At around noon, I began to get worried. While Mohamed sleeps in occasionally, it's never this late.

We didn't have a TV in the room and the Internet didn't seem to be working, which was not surprising given the type of hostel we were staying at and the general Egyptian Internet unreliability, so we had no way of knowing what was happening in Cairo.

I called his mother's cell phone. *Ring, ring. Ring, ring.* Again, I got the same message that her cell phone was turned off.

I called his dad's cell phone. Same issue.

At that point, I became worried. Mohamed sometimes had his phone turned off or forgotten to charge it, but it was very concerning that neither of his parents had their phones on either.

"Helle, I don't know what is going on, but neither Mohamed nor his parents' phones seem to be working," I said.

"That is very strange," she said.

Just then, my cell phone rang with a landline number. While most people in Egypt had a landline, it was very uncommon to use them, so this was definitely unusual.

I picked up the phone.

"Hi, this is Catherine," I said.

"Hey Catherine, this is Saif, from work. Is your cell phone working?" he asked.

"Yes, why wouldn't it be?"

"Well, it seems like the government has somehow shut down the cell phone network. I only tried your cell because I didn't have a landline listed on the phone tree," he said.

"I'm in Luxor with Helle actually. Maybe that is why? What is going on in Cairo? We don't have a TV. And what do you mean they shut down the cell network? How is that even possible?" I said, panic rising in my voice as I processed what he said.

"We don't know. But most of us can't use our cell phones. We think they are trying to limit organizers' ability to communicate. The protests have gotten very large. Are you both safe?" he asked.

"I think so. I mean, we're in a hostel in Luxor. Everything seems to be fine here for now. I just can't believe the government would do that! It feels quite extreme. Maybe we should try to get home quickly," I said.

"Yes, that's probably a good idea. Anyway, if you could call the next person on the phone tree to make sure they are okay."

"Sure, thanks for the call."

Shortly after that phone call, I got another call from a landline, this time from Mohamed.

"Cat? Are you okay? What's going on in Luxor?" he asked, with a clear amount of worry and concern in his voice.

"I'm fine, Helle's fine. We're in the hostel. Things seem to be okay here but getting a bit scared about being so far away from you and Cairo. We just heard about the cell networks being down," I said.

"Yes, I think you both should try and get back to Cairo this afternoon if you can. Things are getting bad here and it would be better if you could be close by."

"Okay, we'll try to get to the Egyptair office and change our ticket. What is happening?" I said.

"There are police and Central Security Forces everywhere. We heard there are clashes between protesters and security forces in Tahrir," he said.

Mohamed lived with his family in downtown Cairo only a kilometer away from Tahrir Square.

"Cat, please stay safe. I love you," he said.

"*Wa ana kaman* (and me too)," I replied as I always do.

All thoughts of the race had vanished, even if my sore legs remained evidence of our accomplishment.

Helle and I exited the hostel to get some food on our way to the Egyptair office onto the main street and ran into a massive demonstration of people walking down the street in the same direction. While nothing compared to the demonstrations in Cairo and other major cities, the crowd seemed to be hundreds of people, carrying signs and chanting.

Many of the chants and slogans soon became ubiquitous.

"*El sha'ab yureed, es-qaat el-nazaam* (The people want the fall of the regime)."

Or simply, "*Irhal (leave)!*"

Helle and I were too consumed with the new goal of getting back to Cairo to fully absorb the pivot in our lives from only a few hours earlier in the day. We went from running a half marathon and romanticizing about running through ancient Egyptian history to panic at being hundreds of miles away from anyone who knew us and wondering if we would have any way to communicate with them.

Egypt had found a new way to keep me on my toes.

We waited for the protesters to walk away from us and turn onto another road

We arrived at the Egyptair office, shaken and running on adrenaline at walking over a kilometer to the office, despite having run twenty-one kilometers hours earlier. We also had forgotten that we had not eaten a proper meal yet.

"Allo, can I help you?" the desk agent asked us.

"*Ahlan wa sahlan.* Yes, we have a return flight to Cairo tomorrow but want to get back as quickly as possible. Can we change the ticket to a flight today?" I asked.

"*Mish mushkila (*no problem), let me have your confirmation information."

He starts typing away furiously on his computer.

"*Mish mushkila.* There is a flight this afternoon and only requires a small change fee. I can book you both on that flight?" he asked.

"*Aiwa, shukran* (Yes, thank you)," I said.

He begins his frantic typing again. He pauses, looks at the screen, and frantically types some more. He stops again, frowns, presses enter several times and then turns to us.

"I'm sorry, something seems to be wrong with the computer. I will have to call the central office in Cairo," he says.

He picks up the phone, and in very fast Arabic that Helle and I only mostly understand, he gives them our information and talks about something being "*bayaz* (broken)."

"I'm very sorry. My colleagues in Cairo were able to make the change, however it appears there is some kind of system issue in Cairo, and they can't get the changes through to me," he says.

"Could we go to the airport and get a new ticket?" I ask.

"Maybe, but they may be having issues too," he said.

We thanked him for his time and went outside, not sure what to do.

"What do you think? Should we just go to the airport? Or should we wait until tomorrow? It's only one more night," I said.

"Agreed, let's just wait until tomorrow," Helle said.

It had not even crossed our mind that what we had experienced was anything bigger than the glitchy Egyptair computer system. *Oh Egypt*, I thought.

We found a restaurant on the Nile to have a long overdue meal; the adrenaline from the last few hours had pushed thoughts of food from our mind for hours, but suddenly, we realized how hungry we were. The midafternoon sun created a streak of gold across the Nile, with the Eastern bank far in the distance. It seemed impossible to contrast the peace of the ever-flowing Nile with the abrupt changes from the past several hours. As we sat there, both of us were working to process what was happening even with the limited information we had about the protests in Cairo that day.

Finally, Helle broke the pensive silence that embraced both of us.

"How are you feeling? Pretty annoying that the Egyptair system was down," she said nervously.

"It's Egypt, the Internet is always glitchy. I'm feeling okay. Just hard to believe the protests haven't been broken up given the number of security forces Mohamed said he saw," I said. "I can't imagine how big that means the protest must have gotten."

"Agreed. I wonder what that means Cairo will be like when we get back," Helle mused. "But it's only one more day. We're going to be fine."

"Yeah, what could possibly happen between now and then," I replied.

After a much-needed nap, Helle and I were getting ready to join the other runners for a pasta dinner several miles away, which was planned by the race organizers. We either were in denial about the impact of the protests or still believed we could have certainty over the future.

I was sitting on the bed looking out the window at the main street, which was mostly emptied from both protesters and the usual tourists. Everything seemed calm.

Then I heard a deep roar of an engine and the window rattled.

"What in the world is that?" Helle asked.

The rumbling got louder.

"Oh my gosh, it's a tank!" I said.

"A tank? Like, a military tank? Why is there a tank on the street?"

"I have no idea. I have never seen one before on the street," I said.

We both watched as tank after tank rolled in front of our second-floor window. Egypt certainly made a show of security, particularly around touristic sites, with police often wielding openly visible rifles. Central Security Forces on the front lines of breaking up protests usually came with full riot gear and their large security trucks not far behind them.

But I had never seen a tank or the presence of the military on the streets in Egypt.

"Why is there a tank on the street? Are they here to keep the peace? Is Mubarak sending in the military to break up the protests? Are they going to use the tanks on protesters?" I wondered out loud.

"I don't know, but this can't be good. I think it also means no pasta dinner," Helle said.

"Ha, yeah. Definitely no pasta dinner," I said.

When we did go down to the lobby of the hostel, we planned to merely cross the street and grab food, but the man behind the front desk informed us a curfew had been put in place. Most hostels and hotels have a security guard or police officer stationed at each entrance, often sitting next to sporadically operational metal detectors. The perception of security around tourist sites were of high importance.

That night, the security guard at the door to the hostel stopped us as we tried to exit the building.

"*Anti rahaya fayn* (where are you going)?" he asked.

"*Ihna ga'aaneen. Ihna rayhena al-ma'ataam dah* (we are hungry. We are going to the restaurant over there)," I replied.

"*Mashy. Lakan al-ma'ataam bes* (okay. But the restaurant only)," he said.

Once we got to the restaurant, the situation finally began hitting us as we shoveled food into our mouths.

"Maybe we should have just gone to the airport this afternoon and gone back to Cairo," I said.

"Maybe. But if things are serious here, I wonder what is happening there," Helle said.

"Good point. I would feel better being in my own apartment though and close to our friends," I said.

"Yes, at least if we were home there would be people who knew us nearby if anything happened," she said.

"Sending tanks to the street seems like a pretty big escalation. I wonder if it will deter protesters or make things worse."

Incredibly, that day had started with nervousness about running a half marathon and ended with nervousness about our physical security because of the protests.

The day did not end there.

We walked into the hostel and noticed a group of men sitting in the courtyard area. We needed to walk past them to get to our room, and as we did, they stared at us in a way that made us feel very uncomfortable. We heard them muttering something to each other in a language neither of us knew. One of them catcalled us as we opened the door to our room.

Two foreign women traveling alone could often attract attention.

When we got to the room, we both looked at each other. Clearly, we felt uncomfortable with our situation. Now, we had to worry about creepy hotel guests too. Helle checked the locks on the door. While we were on edge about the protests, the threat of those men barging into the room while we slept felt much more immediate.

At least sexual harassment could be relied upon to be predictable, I thought to myself.

After reluctantly and fearfully falling asleep, we both were suddenly awakened by the sound of distant gunfire sometime in the middle of the night.

I looked at Helle and went to the window. I couldn't see anything on the street. After many long minutes of listening, we determined the gunfire was far away. We didn't know what to do other than stay where we were.

So, we both turned over and tried our best to get some sleep.

CHAPTER 12:

A QUICK ESCAPE

———

Waking up on January 29th felt like waking up in a dream.

We were both shaken. We had access to our cell phones, but we didn't know for how long. We didn't have Internet. We didn't know a single person in the city other than each other. And the normally bustling tourist city of Luxor quickly began emptying of tourists.

Growing up in Florida, a summer storm often appeared almost out of nowhere turning a sunny, warm day into a black sky filled with rain, thunder, and lightning. Summer storms were as unpredictable as they are severe. The beginning of the revolution felt the same way.

While the main international news organizations focused their cameras on Tahrir Square, protests blossomed in most major cities across the country. Alexandria, Suez, Port Said, and others. Most protests included violent clashes with government forces.

We didn't know it yet, but overnight President Mubarak fired his cabinet while protesters set fire to the National Democratic Party (NDP) headquarters that bordered Tahrir Square. The destruction of the NDP, practically synonymous with Mubarak's regime, felt as impossible as it did symbolic, and it foreshadowed events to come.

The Egyptian military were deployed to secure the Egyptian Museum, home to the largest collection of ancient Egyptian artifacts in the world and a neighbor of the NDP on Tahrir Square, to protect the priceless artifacts. Soon, the extensive mummy collection played host to military generals focused on keeping the peace.

Much would be written about the impact of social media, particularly Twitter and Facebook, in enabling activists and protesters. Others theorized shutting off the cell phone network and limiting Internet encouraged more people to go onto the streets; the streets became the place to gather news and exchange information as much as act as a canvas for Egyptian's frustration with the government.

The Egyptian government was no stranger to censoring the population. In 2010, Freedom House categorized Egypt as "partly free" in its annual Press Freedom Index. Out of all countries in the Middle East and North Africa it ranked fourth but tied for 130rd place with Colombia, Guatemala, and Mexico. Egypt's media landscape included both state-run media channels, radio stations, and newspapers as well as independent and international news outlets.

Most were aware of the unseen, forbidden border of permitted and off-limit topics.

Most of these forbidden topics included questioning the health and strength of Mubarak or his government. In 2007, editors of four independent publications were found guilty of "publishing false information likely to disturb public order" for questioning Mubarak's health (Committee to Protect Journalists, 2007). However, that did not stop speculation and questions from swirling in the Egyptian press in 2010 when the country learned Mubarak, eighty-one at the time, flew to Germany for gall bladder surgery. His presidential term was set to expire in fall of 2011, and some speculated whether he would run for another five-year term or, as many believed he desired, open the door for his son Gamal to run instead (Slackman, 2010).

Denying the conversation in the media could not stop Egyptians' very real frustrations with daily realities.

Egypt felt like it existed at a consistent low boil over the lack of infrastructure, jobs, opportunity, and upward mobility. The steam impacted everyday interactions from fights with taxi drivers over a fare to some real or perceived slight on the street. Getting through the day could feel like a battle. With little government safety net nor financial instruments to allow people to build a future, Egyptians relied on themselves and their families to get them through uncertainty or loss. This forced self-reliance could take a toll on a population scraping to get by.

When the government took away people's ability to communicate, they took away one of the bedrock "services" everyone relied upon. For some, it was the last straw, leading to the unprecedented numbers of Egyptians who took to the streets that Friday, January 28th, later dubbed the "Friday of Anger."

It took Helle and I until sometime Saturday morning to figure out that the Egyptair system issue was not due to spotty Internet but no Internet, and we learned that the Egyptian government figured out how to "shut off the Internet" leading to a 90% drop in data traffic, according to an article in the *New York Times* with the blunt headline "Egypt Cuts Off Most Internet and Cell Service."

Mubarak's willingness to go to extreme measures to stay in power felt dangerous, unpredictable, and terrifying.

Helle and I wanted nothing more than to get back to Cairo — fast. Between the men in our hostel and the events on the street, we felt unsafe and untethered from our support networks in Cairo. Cairo was home. At least there we had access to our own apartments, clean clothes, friends, colleagues, and people who loved us and would help make sure we were okay.

In Luxor, we knew no one.

We were also running out of cash. The banks closed because of the violence on the streets. Helle had thankfully withdrawn some additional cash the day before at a still-functioning ATM. Few places accepted credit cards and, given the communication disruptions, we weren't sure if our credit cards would even work.

As we were getting ready to leave, my cell phone rang.

"Hi Catherine, this is Gamal from work. We are running through the phone tree to make sure everyone is okay after last night. Where are you? Are you safe?" my colleague asked.

"Helle and I are together and safe for now. But we are going to the Luxor Airport to get back to Cairo. We don't feel comfortable being alone here and we're running out of cash."

"Don't come back to Cairo. You should talk to our security team, but there have been reports of gunfire and car-jackings around the Cairo Airport," he said.

Helle and I spent the next hour or so talking to various colleagues and friends about the best plan of action, trying to understand the security situation and the risks involved in returning to Cairo.

Riots and violence overnight had quickly changed the security situation. Multiple police stations were burned or vandalized; Egyptians had little affection for the Egyptian police, often seen as both corrupt and brutal. Reports of the police leaving the streets entirely created a security vacuum that made way for looters and vandalism. Many believed *beltagaya* (hired thugs), likely paid by the Egyptian government, may have instigated at least some of the violence. These facts we pieced together later, that morning we had limited information other than mayhem seemed to have broken out in Cairo.

Mohamed and I talked throughout the morning also trying to decide what we should do. Helle and I did not want to remain in Luxor alone but getting back to Cairo suddenly felt unsafe too. Being two foreign women made us stand out most places in Egypt but being two foreign women in Luxor with no other tourists around with a population expressing decades of anger and frustration made us feel particularly exposed.

"What do you think we should do?" I asked Helle.

"Well, we don't have clean clothes, cash for only a couple more days, and I feel very uncomfortable being here not knowing anyone who could help us if anything happened," she replied.

"Yes, agreed. Plus, it's not like we can just get in a car and drive somewhere. We can't even rent cars, and I don't know if, given everything going on, I'd feel comfortable hiring a driver to take us out of Luxor," I said.

"I do think we need to get out of this hostel. That feels like the more immediate concern. If we go to a nicer hotel, they usually have better security and at least we could have a TV to track what is happening in Cairo," Helle said. She was always incredibly practical and matter of fact.

"Although the nicer hotels could equally be a target. But I agree, I don't like how those men were staring at us. It won't matter what is happening on the street if there is the chance for something happening inside of the hostel."

With that, we made at least one decision to move to a different hotel down the road.

When we got to the hotel, the typical transitory hotel lobby of people waiting to start a vacation and others ending one, was non-existent. Instead, the mood felt closer to panic.

There were some remaining groups of foreign tourists looking anxious and afraid, as their tour guides or handlers barked instructions to gather and get on buses; many tourists to places like Luxor come through tour groups, difficult as it is to navigate Egypt otherwise. There were staff trying to make the guests as comfortable as possible while wearing their own anxieties clearly on their face.

When we walked up to the check-in counter, the front desk attendant seemed surprised we wanted to book a room.

"You're checking-in? Don't you mean checking out?" he asked.

"No, no, we want a room." Helle replied.

"Aren't you part of a tour group? Aren't they getting you home?" he asked, still in disbelief.

"*La'a. Ihna sekna fil-Qahira wa mustsnaneen henna...lama 'al protest* (no, we live in Cairo and are waiting until after the protests)," I replied, realizing at the end of my sentence I didn't know the word in Arabic for protests (yet). Even though he spoke fluent English as most people who work in hotels in Egypt often do, I thought switching to Arabic would make him believe we really wanted a room.

It worked.

"*Mish mushkila* (no problem). I can give you a very good rate, plenty of rooms available," he said.

"Could we have a room that doesn't face the street?" Helle asked. "Just in case."

He apologized in advance that their typical food service would be modified as many hotel workers had not showed up. We were just happy to be in a room with a TV and air conditioning, small luxuries.

We spent the next several hours glued to the TV, finally able to see the images of the protests that were upending the country. The news panned to images of streets that I walked daily. In Tahrir Square, I could name most of the stores and restaurants in the panoramic view on TV. I could see the luggage store I bought the suitcase I currently had with me. Down that street was *Koshary Tahrir,* where I first figured out how to order Egyptian street food. Right off the square was my favorite local crafts store that I frequented for authentic gifts for family back home. And of course, there was American University in Cairo where I had studied and met Mohamed. The place I called home.

The juxtaposed hopeful image of hundreds of thousands of Egyptians taking every available space in Tahrir Square and squares across the country with the destruction around the city from the violence the previous night were difficult to process. Despite the very real images, the whiplash from normality left me in utter disbelief.

Eventually, though, we needed to get something to eat.

Helle is one of the most practical people I have ever met. She is diligent in everything she does, including the numerous hobbies she has picked up over the years from running to triathlons to ballroom dancing. When we decided to run the half-marathon together, she pulled together a training plan and held us militantly to the schedule to achieve our target race time; she analyzed our splits after each run to determine the next run's pace. She always makes a plan and a backup plan, which she believes stems from her native Danish culture of expecting and planning for the worst as a way to manage expectations.

The events of the past few days tested even her worst-case scenario planning.

She suggested we should walk to the more Egyptian part of town to get to a proper grocery store to stock up on food supplies in case we couldn't leave the hotel that evening. She also suggested we look for something, anything, that we could use to defend ourselves if needed.

We had to walk over a kilometer and a half (which I knew was a mile with my newly found metric system-fluency) to a food market. As we walked, we saw the aftermath of the noise we had heard from a distance the previous night. Many of the storefronts on the main road were either boarded up or had been broken into. Debris littered the street. And even though it was Saturday, typically a busy weekend day, the streets were practically empty. We saw almost no foreign tourists, very uncommon.

We made it to the market and loaded up on canned tuna, cookies, chips, cheese, whatever we could find that we thought would last a few days. We asked the store owner if he sold a pocketknife. He did not.

In a decision that only seemed comical much later, we purchased a can of bug spray as a kind of substitute for pepper spray.

As the clerk calculated manually how much we owed, we heard screaming and chanting outside. Someone ran into the store and yelled something in Arabic. We didn't understand most of what he said, but the urgency in his voice was clear. The shopkeeper told us in a mixture of English and Arabic that we needed to get out of there right away because there was a large protest coming, and there were reports of Central Security Forces clashing with protesters. Immediately after his explanation, we heard a sound of what could have been either gunfire or tear gas canisters being shot, almost to emphasize his point.

We exited the shop quickly, carrying our food. The street was mostly empty. Down the street we could see the protest several blocks away. A new and strange smell hung in the air. That smell, which would soon get added to the tapestry of Cairo smells, we soon learned was tear gas.

Without knowing which direction we were going, we just started half walking, half running away from the protests. We made turns that we thought generally would lead us back to the hotel. Trying to put as much distance between ourselves and the protest as possible left us no time to pull out a map to make sure we were walking in the exact right direction.

When we got back to the hotel and caught our breath, we agreed we needed to get out of Luxor if going on a simple walk to the grocery store could feel dangerous.

We still assumed if we left Luxor we would return to Cairo. Mohamed was in Cairo, and we were weeks away from getting married. The apartment we would live in together after the wedding, that we were still furnishing and making our home, was in Cairo. The past three years of my life were in Cairo, and my entire adult post-university life, which felt in some ways like my whole life. My friends, my job, my hangouts, my memories all were in Cairo. It felt impossible that in twenty-four hours anything about my life could have changed so much to make Cairo unsafe.

Helle and I called one of our work managers to tell them our intention to get on the next flight back to Cairo. Instead, we were told the office was chartering a flight to take any staff or family, Egyptian or non-Egyptian, to Dubai where we had an office. We heard that groups of vigilantes either taking advantage of the fluid security situation or potentially encouraged by the regime as a tool to scare people into staying home were terrorizing certain neighborhoods, particularly

Christian neighborhoods, with several staff having had groups show up at their doorstep looking for trouble.

They told us we needed to find a direct flight out of Egypt from Luxor and not transit in Cairo because of the uncertain security situation; they were not sure we could safely get from the airport back home. Under normal circumstances that is not easy because so many flights transit through Cairo from Luxor. In this environment, that guidance was even more difficult to follow as many international carriers began canceling flights into and out of the country.

We agreed to stay that night in Luxor while they researched potential options. Helle and I began brainstorming our own solutions too. Could we stay with Helle's parents in Denmark? Or my aunt and uncle in London? Without saying it out loud, Helle and I decided no option would include us separating. We had gone from colleagues and casual friends, little more than running buddies, to each other's life rafts.

I called Mohamed to talk about what we should do.

"Hey, Helle and I are looking into flights to Europe. But I just want to come back to Cairo," I said.

"No, you cannot come back to Cairo. You and Helle need to leave Egypt," he said.

"Why? What is going on?" I asked. I obviously saw the images on the news but the edge in his voice told me he had witnessed more than large demonstrations of people or not atypical clashes between protesters and security forces.

"You need to get out of Egypt. I need to know that at least you're safe," he said.

"I know but I need to know you're safe too," I said.

"Please, just find a way out of Egypt."

I could tell he was holding back details. But whatever he had witnessed made him desperate for me to leave. We both worked at the same organization so he could evacuate to Dubai too.

"Okay, but why don't you go to Dubai with work? Maybe Helle and I can figure out how to get there from Luxor. At least we can be together," I said.

"Let me think about it. I don't know if I can leave my parents and brother."

Ultimately, he said he would meet me in Dubai. I felt relieved but also guilty for making him chose between staying with his family and country and staying with me. I felt so panicked after the last couple days the guilt did not rise as far to the surface.

The following day, Sunday January 30th, was a whirlwind. Helle and I spent the day on the phone with a variety of colleagues who were all trying to figure out how to first find a flight direct out of Luxor, purchase a plane ticket, and then figure out how to get us the ticket given the Internet was still down.

I also talked to my mom, who was helping plan our wedding.

"Hey Cat, are you getting out of Egypt? Is Mohamed? Should we cancel the wedding?" she rapidly asked.

"Yes, yes, and I have no idea," I replied.

"But we need to tell the guests something, it's only six weeks away."

"Well, we're not going to get any of the deposits back anyway so let's just wait to see what happens," I said, assuming (hoping) everything would be back to normal by then.

In between these frantic phone calls, Helle and I paused periodically to consider how drastically our world and how Egypt had changed. Despite Egypt's multitude of challenges, and harassment notwithstanding, Egypt generally felt safe.

Part of that safety came from the tight grip of the police, but the bigger part was simply there were people everywhere at every time of day. Walking around downtown Cairo, even late at night, there were almost always people walking around; Cairo gives New York City a run for its money for the title of the "city that doesn't sleep."

Although the sexual harassment had a constant presence in my day-to-day life, I never felt worried or concerned about walking home late at night alone or taking a taxi by myself across the city at any time of day. Suddenly, that safety and blanket of protection was gone. Helle and I debated how best to even get to the airport or walk a few blocks to get food.

That was difficult enough to absorb. The idea that Mubarark's regime and presidency could be coming to an end still felt a long way off. At most, we surmised, he would be forced to agree to more democratic elections or allow for greater political dissent and political activism. Even that "small" change would be progress.

With no ability to find our own flight out of Egypt, we waited while our families researched different options. While we discussed what might happen next, my phone rang. The director of our entire region, a man I had only gotten all-staff emails from, answered.

"Hi, is this Catherine? This is Yiorgos," he said.

"Um, hi. Yes, this is Catherine. Um, how are you?" nervous to be speaking with someone so senior in my organization.

"I have been helping to figure out how to get you and Helle out of Egypt."

"Oh, um, thank you?" I replied, confused he even knew who we were.

"I found you a ticket that goes direct from Luxor to Doha and then to Dubai. I assume you both have your passports with you?"

"Yes, we do."

"Great, now I'm going to need your names and passport numbers so I can purchase the ticket. Then, you'll need to find a fax machine so I can fax you the tickets since I can't email them to you," he said.

"Okay sure, we can figure that out," I said.

We found out later that the director of the region had become personally involved in getting staff out of Cairo and had taken an interest in solving the puzzle of how to get the two foreign women out of Luxor. From purchasing our plane tickets to helping charter a flight out of Cairo, he had insisted on helping get everyone out safely who wanted to leave.

We gave him the information he needed. Then we had to figure out how to find a fax machine in the hotel.

Egypt might have been behind the times on technology in a myriad of ways, but even they didn't use fax machines anymore; thankfully, Egypt has a strong focus on preserving antiquities, otherwise we may not have found a fax machine buried in a box under a stack of papers in the hotel gift shop. Even more thankfully, the thing still worked.

The ticket was for the following day, Monday January 31st. The airline had warned Yiorgos when he purchased the ticket that there was a good chance the flight might get cancelled. The security situation changed hour-to-hour and they could not guarantee the plane would take off until it was basically in the air.

Helle asked what plan B was if the flight didn't take off. We were told to hope that the plane took off.

That night was uneventful in Luxor although protests continued around the country. It felt like the entire country was taking a deep breath and was waiting for the Egyptian government to make their next move. Protesters in Tahrir Square had been camping out, setting up tents, and creating a mini city inside the perimeter of the square equipped with checkpoints, entertainment, and medical stations for protesters injured in clashes with security forces. Protesters made it clear they were there to stay.

Images of Tahrir Square, packed with Egyptians, flooded televisions around the world as political commentators theorized about the end outcome. It felt too early to feel hopeful for real change, but the massive numbers of people flooding streets around Egypt made the underlying tension and anger visible. On Egyptian state media, in contrast, images of packed squares and vocal protesters did not exist. Instead, there were only images of a peaceful, ever flowing Nile with news hosts hell-bent on ignoring the protests.

We woke up the morning of January 31st feeling optimistic about being able to get out of Luxor. I called Mohamed who was making preparation to leave with many of our colleagues to meet me in Dubai.

Getting off the phone, I began to feel more guilty for asking him to come to Dubai when I knew he wanted to continue going to the protests and stay with his family. I also really wanted him to be safe and for us to be together. The thought of being away from him while events in Egypt continued to unfold felt impossible to consider, particularly when the last few days felt like torture knowing he stood somewhere among the sea of Egyptians standing in Tahrir Square; I felt terrified something might happen to him.

Helle and I packed our incredibly few belongings (including the bug spray) and had the hotel call a taxi for us; typically, the street would be filled with taxis and cars, but the streets were practically empty.

The ride from the hotel to the airport allowed us to get a more complete picture of the changes in the city from only a few days earlier — the day our top priority included finishing a race. The city was a ghost town — debris on the road, stores boarded up, no tourists, and few people were walking around the streets. We passed the first tank just down the road from the hotel. Like a scene from a post-apocalyptical movie; I half expected a zombie to come limping down the street.

When we arrived at the airport, two tanks flanked the entrance. We were stopped by the military when we arrived at the entrance to check our passports and inquire about our destination. They also inspected our tickets. After several questions about who we were and why we were leaving, they let us through.

When we got into the airport, small crowds of people surrounded each of the airline desks in varying stages of stress and anxiety. Most seemed desperately looking for flights to take them out of the country. We uneventfully checked in and made it through security despite a minor argument about trashing the bug spray. Our flight was on time and on schedule.

I called Mohamed once we were through security and told him we were safe. He was at a hotel near the Cairo Airport with many of our other colleagues who were also evacuating to Dubai. I would see him the next day in Dubai once their plane landed.

We knew it was likely the last time we would talk until I saw him the next day. Helle and I wouldn't arrive in Dubai until the early hours of the morning given a long layover in Doha. His cell phone was still not working, making communication difficult. I was more relaxed knowing I would see him the next day and that we would both be safely together.

Neither Helle nor I really internalized we were leaving until the wheels were up on the plane and we were in the air;

I felt so anxious I insisted on keeping my small duffel bag, with my few possessions inside, on my lap, which caused a debate with the flight attendant who relented. Even after safely landing in Dubai, we insisted on sharing a room, both of us needed each other to feel safe, protected. We also still had most of the food we purchased at the grocery store a couple days before, although I could not explain why we clung to those cans of tuna and packages of bread.

We woke up the next morning in disbelief. We did not know how long we would remain in Dubai, and we naively assumed it would only be for a few days. So, we put on our running clothes and decided to go for a run. We had several hours before our colleagues would land in Dubai, and we could meet them at a different hotel across the city.

Halfway through our run, my cell phone rang. The number was coming from an Egyptian landline. Mohamed, who should have been on a plane at that moment, answered.

"Hey Cat," he began, "I decided to stay in Cairo."

I felt like my heart sank below my feet.

CHAPTER 13:

A NEW BEGINNING

———

I stood stock still in the middle of the sidewalk. Helle had realized I had stopped running and doubled back to see what was going on.

"I know I said I was going to come to Dubai, but once I knew you were safe, I felt like I needed to stay," Mohamed said.

I didn't answer immediately. I felt like a large rock had suddenly appeared inside my throat that was making it impossible to say anything.

"Catherine, are you there?" Mohamed asked.

"Yes, I'm here. But you're not," I said, somewhat dramatically.

"I know. We heard gunfire all night after protesters tried to get into the Ministry of Interior. I didn't want to tell you before so you wouldn't worry, but I felt like I couldn't leave my parents alone in case something happened."

I sighed.

"No, you're right. You should stay in Cairo to be with your family. I know if it was my country I would want to be there too."

"So, you're not mad?" Mohamed asked.

"I'm not mad. I'm scared. I don't know what is going to happen or when I'm going to see you."

"I know. I love you. I'll call you every day," he promised.

"*Wa ana kaman* (so do I). I'll talk to you later."

We hung up.

I felt like I had been punched in the stomach in the middle of a deep, cleansing breath. The relief I had felt only minutes earlier at the prospect of seeing Mohamed vanished instantly. I found it almost impossible to run back to the hotel. Every other minute I had to pause because I got so choked up with fear for Mohamed's safety that I couldn't breathe. I had no idea when I would see him again, if he and his family would be safe, or what would happen in Egypt.

The government seemed too strong to go quickly or willingly, and the protesters seemed equally as immovable in their resolve. So, what happens when an immovable object is struck by an unstoppable force? Two people who love each other get stuck thousands of miles apart.

We made it back to the hotel, changed, and watched as much news as possible to pass the time and to feel less far away from home. The Egyptian government seemed to be running its multi-pronged, battle-tested playbook: create fear and distrust among the population, use the state-owned media to create alternative narratives, and position itself as the sole party able to establish stability and peace. However, the playbook decades in the making did not seem to be working this time.

Part one of the playbook: create fear and distrust. Police left the streets, seemingly on orders of someone in the government, and were replaced with looters who caused chaos across cities. Neighborhood groups formed to defend the streets and homes from these vigilantes. At the same time, there were reports of prisoners breaking out of overcrowded Egyptian prisons — or being strategically released to sow fear among the population.

Part two, create alternative narratives: journalists were attacked or expelled from the country while the Egyptian propaganda apparatus tried to position the protesters as foreign-influenced agents of Islamic extremism, rather than anything but what they were — everyday citizens. In one of the more bizarre examples of the desperation of the Egyptian government, a narrative emerged the protesters were foreign agents. The proof? Protesters were seen eating Kentucky Fried Chicken, one of several American fast-food restaurants with a storefront on Tahrir Square. This became quick fodder for Egyptian jokes and memes, with protesters posting pictures eating KFC or with dropped sandwiches on the ground. Others mocked-up Mubarak to look like Colonel Sanders, the KFC mascot. Incidents like this gave instant material to comedic websites like *El Koshary Today*, an online Egyptian version of *The Onion*.

Part three: establish stability and peace and take credit for doing so. Mubarak made concessions and gave televised speeches to bolster the image of the regime and remind Egyptians, and the international community, of the importance of Egyptian stability — Mubarak's attempt to connect the dots between Egyptian stability and his government's ability to continue in power.

However, protestors continued to defy recently established curfews and remained camped out overnight, growing in numbers. They did not seem deterred by fear and intimidation. They did not need media to explain the narrative, in fact, they were the narrative. Comedy and jokes flamed dissent. Mubarak's arguments that only he could provide stability did not work. Decades under Mubarak's smoke and-mirrors reforms were proof that words alone were not enough, only action.

The protests included Egyptians from all backgrounds. Members of the Muslim Brotherhood protested alongside liberal, secular political parties. Young, barely adult activists who were born and raised under Mubarak stood shoulder-to-shoulder with Egyptians who had experienced all three modern day Egyptian presidents. Upper class Egyptian voices melded with Egyptians barely making a living wage to call for the fall of the regime. Women joined men in camping out overnight to hold Tahrir Square. Muslims and Christians prayed together, protected one another. Many of my Egyptian friends who attended the protests described them as an equalizer across all the multitude of divisions within the country. They described how Tahrir Square became a community where ideas were exchanged, services were provided, and relationships formed; the protests created unity among groups that infrequently had opportunities to interact.

Meanwhile, "the people demand the fall of the regime" and simply "leave" became the battle cries of protesters across the city. Both demands would have been nearly unthinkable for any-sized group of individuals to say out loud in Egypt before, but the people of Egypt were now screaming for change at the top of their lungs. The power was on their side.

As Egyptians and the world waited for what would happen next, the Egyptian military was the biggest wild card. Would they continue to support Mubarak who came from its ranks? Or would they side with the Egyptian people? They chose the people. The military refused to participate in attacks on protesters and, instead, became a protective barrier between protesters and security forces. Mohamed Hussein Tantawi, Egypt's Minister of Defense and Commander in Chief of the Egyptian Armed Forces, visited Tahrir Square in a show of support for the Egyptian people. The imagery from the revolution often included protesters standing in front of tanks or military service members, co-existing together as part of the landscape of the revolution. Many pictures from that time included Egyptians standing and smiling in front of tanks with protest banners draped over them like party decorations.

Most Egyptians saw the military as the neutral third party, the arbiter of peace, and the last and best hope of facilitating a conversation between activists demanding change and the regime demanding to remain in place.

A consortium of Egyptian activist groups called the National Association for Change led by Mohamed El Baradei, a former Director General of the International Atomic Energy Agency (IAEA) and Egyptian diplomat who supported reform of the government, called officially for Mubarak to step down and for a new government. However, despite the massive protests, Egyptians remained on the fence about whether a new government or a set of promised reforms should be the goal. Some were merely calling for democratic reforms, less media censorship, and greater freedom of speech and expression. The staying power and size of the protests alone was an achievement in a country where protesting could mean getting arrested or worse; the protests proved cracks in Mubarak's hold on the country existed.

The real question that felt far from having a concrete answer was this: what would happen next?

Meanwhile, Helle and I were waiting for our colleagues to arrive in Dubai on a plane that did not include Mohamed. We again packed our few possessions together (including the cans of tuna fish) to move across the city to a hotel where we would be staying for the foreseeable future.

When our colleagues eventually arrived, a group of about one hundred including their families, we all gathered around the outdoor deck in the hotel for an impromptu "meeting." The group included the Director of our region who had bought Helle and I's plane ticket. It also included close to all the expatriates in the office (some had chosen to go to whichever country they called home instead) and many Egyptians, mostly those who had small children or were Egyptian Christians.

Fear, stress, and uncertainty were written across everyone's faces. Over the coming days we swapped stories of our experiences over those both long and short days since the protests began. Some people witnessed graphic violence in front of their homes as people (likely government-hired thugs or plain clothes police) tried looting shops or breaking into people's homes. Others saw fights break out in their streets. Some expats who lived in more removed or expat-majority parts of the city did not witness the more graphic imagery of the past several days, but their families seemed shaken by the abrupt departure from their homes.

The Regional Director spoke, he gave an overview of the situation on the ground, the plan for our time in Dubai, and acknowledged the range of emotions and experiences we all had. Hearing our boss talk about feelings and emotions felt like a large departure from normal. My colleagues suddenly seemed like full, three-dimensional humans divorced of their titles or hierarchy in the organization, standing with their scared spouses or children. The Regional Director acknowledged some of the unique experiences the staff had over the past week or so.

Perhaps the Director felt a connection to me because he had been on the phone with Helle and I for quite some time trying to get us out of the country because he looked right at me and said, "Catherine, he's going to be okay," a reference to Mohamed who he knew remained in Egypt.

I was going for an appearance of stoicism, but my stress and fear was obvious. I do not cry easily or often, but the mention of Mohamed popped the bubble of adrenaline I had created to get through the last several days and punctured whatever shield I created between myself and reality, and I burst into tears.

Helle led me away from the meeting, and I sobbed quietly back in the hotel hallway.

The list of things I didn't know about Egypt's future, so closely tied to my own, seemed innumerable. How long would we remain in Dubai? When could we safely return to Egypt? What would the government do next? Would Mohamed and his family stay safe? When would I see him again? Even while I stood safely 1500 miles away, it felt impossible to disentangle the fear for Mohamed and my other Egyptian friends from my own. I wanted to jump on the next flight back to Egypt because being close to the situation would release me from the uncertainty, but the logical part of me knew that my presence in Egypt would not be helpful for anyone other than myself.

Our upcoming wedding felt far from what I was capable of thinking about, and thoughts of flower arrangements, music, and seating assignments was impossible to believe would even be necessary on February 1, 2011.

Meanwhile, protests had similarly erupted in several other countries across the Middle East, as if Tunisia and now Egypt splintered the remaining dam keeping the flood of frustration and anger of people across the region. Each country had a unique set of circumstances, politics, and grievances, but those differences did not stop the water of change from immersing the region in uprising.

At that point, Tunisia served as a model for a swift departure of a longtime strongman. However, Mubarak's hold on power felt stronger due to his support from the Egyptian military and close relationships with the US and other Western governments. Few Middle Eastern experts at that point predicted a swift resignation or a resignation at all.

Then came the night of February 2nd, eight days after the protests first began.

On February 1st, Mubarak had made his second public speech since the protests began. He committed he would not run for re-election and would create term limits. However, he also set up the choice for Egyptians as one between "chaos and stability" — even though his government had instigated much of the instability by taking extreme measures like turning the Internet and cell phone network off and seemingly ordering the numerous attacks on peaceful protests by police (Kortam, 2013).

Mubarak's regime had long tried to create the choice for Egyptians as one between safety and chaos, and between a certain, if not dim, economic future for most and economic uncertainty. But then an incident that continues to baffle as to both inspiration and objective occurred that changed everything.

Helle and I continued to share a room and sat on our couch on February 2nd flipping between BBC, CNN International, and Al Jazeera trying to piece together events in real time from three different camera angles. Most coverage remained the same — panoramic shots of Tahrir Square, occasional coverage of other cities, and video of some of the aftermath of scuffles around the country.

Suddenly, there was movement on the screen near the entrance to Tahrir Square near the Egyptian Museum.

I turned to Helle and said, "Are those *camels*?"

"I think so," said Helle in similar disbelief.

"As if it wasn't hard enough to convince people Egyptians don't regularly ride camels," I said, not realizing what was about to happen.

It took another minute or so before we realized these camel- and horse-riding men also had long swords in their hands and were actively battling with the protesters on the ground.

We watched in horror as grisly images of protesters being beaten, trampled, and slashed at with weapons appeared on the screen. In that moment, no one knew who these men were, but it seemed pretty obvious they were not on the side of the protesters.

I watched with a knot in my stomach because I knew that Mohamed stood somewhere in the square that day.

Since cell phone service had mostly returned, I picked up the phone to call him.

I called. No answer.

I called again. No answer.

I must have called dozens of times as I watched the battles emerging on the screen from multiple points around the square. Protesters began throwing Molotov cocktails to ward off the attackers. As a result, one of the buildings lining the square caught fire.

Finally, sometime late in the evening, my cell phone rang. Mohamed was on the line.

"Hey Cat, I can't talk for long, but I wanted to let you know that I'm safe," he said.

"Where are you? Are you home? Are you hurt? What is going on!"

"I was in the square taking pictures and had stopped to have lunch at my friends' apartment over-looking Tahrir when we heard the chanting die down and a different kind of noise begin. We went to the window and saw a bunch of people on horses and camels enter the square from Abdel Moniem Riad. They had weapons and started beating protesters. It went on for hours," he said. "But I'm at a friends' apartment on the square. I can't get home right now so I'm planning to stay the night."

"But who were the men who entered the square?"

"Some are saying they worked at tourist sites like the pyramids and were paid to come and cause trouble, but who knows."

"I'm so glad you're okay and safe."

"I am, but a lot of people aren't," he said.

"Please just call me when you get home tomorrow," I begged.

"I will, I love you."

"*Wa ana kaman*," I replied.

I could see the building he was in on my TV screen. I flipped from channel to channel to try and see that building, like a sports fan convinced watching the game could alter the outcome. The video reels from that day began getting replayed on the news and visuals of protesters using chunks of pavement dug from the street to hurl in the direction of the attack filled the screen. The videos were violent, gruesome, and chaotic.

Eventually, Helle suggested I try and get some sleep. I knew I could not help even if something happened, but it felt like the only thing I could do was to keep watching the news.

I ended up falling asleep on the couch with the TV on that night, not knowing if Mohamed was safe.

The events of that day become known as the "Camel Battle," an incident Egyptian friends and analysts years later would reference as a crucial turning point. The group of pro-Mubarak men riding horses and camels, wielding swords and other weapons, rode into Tahrir Square and brutally attacked protesters. Marches from other parts of the city came in from other entry points, led by various pro-Mubarak members of Parliament and government officials. In the end, 11 people were reported dead and over six hundred injured (Fathi, 2012).

The impact of the wonton violence and the images of Egyptians fighting Egyptians, served as a wakeup call and a galvanizing moment that moved public opinion swiftly within the country. It demonstrated the commitments made by Mubarak only the previous day would not be honored, and that promises of reforms or greater democratic freedoms were only words The patience of the population evaporated. Egyptian friends indicated the mood following the Camel Battle suddenly shifted and united protesters and their supporters behind the idea for Mubarak to immediately step down (France 24, 2011).

International support, including American support, of Mubarak similarly began evaporating. Statements from President Obama shifted from more vague statements about the importance of peaceful protests to more statements that seemed to indicate an assumption Mubarak would soon resign. Mubarak seemed to have gotten metaphorically slapped on the hand by the international community for the violence of those couple days. For a leader like him, who very much tried to be part of the international community, I'm sure the rebuke by leaders around the world stung.

The next week was a bit of a blur. Helle and I went into our Dubai office to attempt to work along with many other colleagues. We spent the hours we weren't trying to work glued to the news. I was able to talk to a few Egyptian friends who remained in Cairo. Some went down to the square to protest while others stayed close to home. It felt like Egypt was again holding its breath (again) waiting for what suddenly felt inevitable — for Mubarak to step down.

Meanwhile, protests began or continued in Libya, Syria, Yemen, and even Jordan. The Western media began describing the protests across the Middle East as a collective energy and a wave of pent-up frustration at economic stagnation, limited opportunities, and a dearth of freedoms erupting in an avalanche of activism, which was surprising considering protests of any kind seemed unthinkable only weeks earlier.

The courage of people across the Arab world to take to the street and demand change cannot be overstated. Most Middle Eastern governments explicitly make protesting illegal and use numerous other tactics to censor free speech from blocking websites, limiting independent media and journalists, to forcing the exile of dissidents. Violence, police brutality, extended imprisonments without due process, and even torture were frequent tools by leaders across the region for those who dare to dissent.

Egypt was no different.

After several more days of binge-watching the news, life needed to go on. We needed to buy groceries to eat, we needed to buy clothes to wear — Helle and I left Egypt with only two changes of clothes. I felt that doing anything close to routine felt forced and an acknowledgement that going back to Cairo would not happen quickly; Helle and I refused to buy enough groceries for more than a few days at a time because we did not want to admit we would be in Dubai for any longer than that. I initially balked at the idea of buying more clothes, insistent I would be back in my Cairo apartment shortly.

But life went on because it had to.

I talked to Mohamed daily, worrying constantly about his safety and the safety of his family. They felt the immediate impacts of the protests given their proximity to Tahrir Square. Despite the imminent countdown to our wedding,

Mohamed and I did not talk about it. I held out hope there would be enough resolution for it to be possible even though with each passing day that seemed less likely. The apartment Mohamed and I were meant to move into together after we were married was unfinished — we had left tasks like picking the kitchen cabinets and new kitchen appliances for the last minute. Our life together was in limbo and uncertainty about how or when we could be together was often the unspoken part of our conversations.

At the same time, Egypt became introduced to new names of activists. Activists like Wael Ghonim, a Google marketing manager and, previously, the anonymous creator of the Facebook popular page "We are All Khaled Said," became widely known. He was arrested and tortured by Egyptian police for eleven days during the revolution and, following his release, rocketed to fame internationally becoming the poster child for social media activism (Ghonim, 2018).

During the revolution, there was an explosion of music. Artists like Cairokee, Wust El Balad, and Ramy Essam wrote songs and created music videos shot from within Tahrir Square. They described the heroism and objectives of the protesters. Their lyrics became the rallying cry for Egyptians, the voices of revolution.

Bassem Yousef, previously a cardiothoracic surgeon, began a series of YouTube videos satirizing the Mubarak regime — all while attending to injured protesters in Tahrir Square during those eighteen days. His videos became so popular that he eventually was given own comedy show called *El Bernamag* (The program) and was often referred to as the "Egyptian Jon Stewart." He was a guest on Jon Stewart's *The Daily Show,* and Jon Stewart was a guest on his show. *El Bernamag* followed a similar format to *The Daily Show* but was completely revolutionary in Egypt where dissent and criticism, even comedic, was forbidden (Paget, 2018).

Egypt is well-known in the Arabic speaking world for its film, television, and music industry, producing many of the shows and music that are enjoyed across the Middle East. This explosion in artistic freedom of expression gave emotional depth to the revolution and allowed Egyptians to tell their own story outside of the twenty-four--hour news cycle.

And then, without warning on February 11th, only eighteen days after the protests began, Mubarak stepped down.

Helle had badgered me into going to the mall to buy a dress that I hoped to wear for Mohamed and I's rehearsal dinner, if we were even able to hold the wedding. We were at the mall when we heard the news on a TV playing in a restaurant. We caused quite a scene as we hugged and cried (loudly) with joy.

It felt unreal, historic, inevitable, and incredible — all at the same time.

Egyptians had organized, gone out to the streets at great personal risk, asked for change, and achieved it. Immediately after the news, Egyptians flooded into squares around the country to celebrate together. In that moment, on that day, celebration and hope felt like the only emotions possible. Perhaps a new, bright future for Egypt was possible. Egyptians had proven to the world and to themselves that change was possible. The transfer of power included violence and great personal sacrifice, but it happened.

On that day, it was possible to forget the hard work, hard decisions, and courage that would be required to cement the gains made during the revolution.

On that day, it was possible to forget that this was just another beginning.

CHAPTER 14:

AN UNCLEAR PATH

Now that over-turning a dictator could be checked off the to-do list, Mohamed and I could again focus on wedding planning.

The days and weeks after Mubarak stepped down remained riddled with questions about the security situation in Egypt.

How would pro-Mubarak forces within the government react?

How would his supporters react, particularly given their attack during the Camel Battle?

Could the military reinstitute law and order on the streets?

Was it safe to be back in Egypt?

I remained in Dubai for a couple weeks while my organization's security team evaluated the security situation. I returned to Cairo for a whirlwind twenty-four hours where I moved out of my apartment that I had left without knowing I was leaving permanently, briefly saw Mohamed, and then boarded a flight to the US for our wedding. Mohamed followed a couple of weeks later as planned, despite the continued variability in commercial air travel out of the Cairo International Airport.

One wedding detail Mohamed and I had long debated included which song to use for our first dance; we struggled to find a song that felt meaningful to both of us. The revolution clarified our decision. We decided on "*Sout Al Horeya* (Voice of freedom*)*" created by members of the Egyptian rock bands Cairokee and Wust El-Balad during the revolution, about the revolution. The music video, filmed in the middle of Tahrir Square, showcased the full diversity of Egyptians: children alongside older Egyptians, Muslims praying next to Christians, women wearing and not wearing hijabs, men in both traditional and modern clothing. The music video includes Egyptian protesters mouthing the lyrics to the song. The lyrics connect the multitude of voices coming from Tahrir Square. The most striking part of the video to me is that most people are smiling and laughing. Joy is evident in their faces at the expected change they were creating for themselves, their country, and their future; the hope on Egyptians' faces in the video still makes me tear up to see.

It felt exactly right.

In the two months before the wedding, we spent less than twenty-four hours together. Instead of arguing over seating arrangements or which shelves we would each get in the closet, we had only had snapshots of conversations when technology allowed. We were supposed to be thinking about the future, and instead, we were weighed down with the heaviness of the present.

The relief I felt when he landed in the Orlando International Airport and the joy in being together eclipsed any pre-wedding jitters; the uncertainty of the revolution made us feel more than certain about the decision to spend the rest of our lives together.

It felt like the easiest decision in the world.

We got married, as planned, on March 12, 2011, in my hometown of Palm Coast, Florida in an interfaith ceremony overlooking the ocean.

Many of my family and friends had not met Mohamed until the wedding since we both lived in Egypt for the entirety of our relationship. While of course they wanted to get to know him, questions about the Egyptian revolution were the first questions he got asked. All the press attention surrounding the Egyptian revolution and what had been dubbed the "Arab Spring" suddenly made Egypt and Egyptians heroes. So much so that even my family and friends who remained skeptical about my relationship with Mohamed suddenly were filled with nothing but awe-inspired questions about the ability of Egyptians to force Mubarak's resignation. While I welcomed the change of heart, it felt off that the revolution created it.

After our wedding and honeymoon, we returned to Egypt to figure out how to live together, just as Egypt was similarly figuring out how to live together in a post-Mubarak country.

The Egypt we returned to was not the one we knew in late January 2011. In the aftermath of the revolution, a floodgate of new political characters competed for power and control over the narrative of the country. Prior to the revolution, Mubarak and his regime had controlled this narrative to a large degree through the media, centering on the importance of stability and incremental progress. Yes, there were opposition groups like the Muslim Brotherhood, the Wafd, or more recent activist groups relying on Facebook to gather support, but these groups inconsistently participated in or won seats in Parliament much less were able to seriously sway the political conversation.

Mubarak was the story and a story with one angle. Until now.

Suddenly, headlines in Egyptian newspapers were critical of Mubarak, the major figures in his regime, the police, and any number of other former power brokers in the country. Even the military was not off limits. Young activist leaders, previously unknown Egyptians like Wael Ghonim, Asmaa Mahfouz, Ramy Essam, Esraa Abdel Fattah, Ahmed Douma, Wael Abbas, Ahmed Maher, became stars with access to the biggest megaphones in the country — the press. Mohamed El Baredei, the former head of the IAEA and the person many believed would unite the country in the next presidential election, actively pushed for change and criticized the former regime.

If this were a Hollywood film, the credits would roll where the story arc of an unlikely hero overcoming the odds has been completed. Instead, this was the ending of one part in a multi-part series with an unknowable number of volumes. The studio wanted to continue making money for as long as possible by producing multiple chapters, re-making the same movie with different actors, and then announcing a "multi-verse," an incomprehensible term that seems to just mean "same part, different actor." This was more or less what was happening in Egypt post-revolution. Many of the same "characters" re-made themselves for volume two.

The Muslim Brotherhood formed a political party called the Freedom and Justice Party. Khairat Shater, the presumptive presidential nominee, became a name anyone following the news soon knew. The young, mainly secular activists struggled to consolidate or come up with a strategy of how to create an organized political movement or select a leader. Instead, they opted to back some emerging players. Members of Mubarak's regime, members of Parliament, and former government officials also were jockeying for a piece, albeit slimmer piece, of the political pie. Immediately after Mubarak stepped down, the military remained in control of the country but pledged to turn power over to a civilian government. Who would lead that government was anyone and everyone's guess.

The "revolution" did not end when Mubarak resigned. Mubarak may have been the head, but the neck and body could thrash around and exist without it — this body was much more like a hydra, capable of reproducing multiple heads that would snap at one another for dominance. The Egyptian protesters may have thought that by chanting "the people want the fall of the regime" that this inherently meant Mubarak's resignation would indeed bring down the regime, but the regime, the systems of power that could quickly subjugate a population, were not completely synonymous with Mubarak. Too many people benefited from the system he created to give up easily.

Mohamed and I arrived back in Egypt after our honeymoon to a changed Egypt. The streets, pollution, traffic, markets, bars and night clubs, friends, restaurants, and taxis all remained the same, but you could sense an entire mood shift, like Egypt herself had woken up on the different side of the bed. She did her hair differently, she sang in the shower, and she had a bounce in her step, even if her eyes darted around more frequently, looking for danger around every corner. She was optimistic, but cautiously so. She was hopeful, but with hesitancy. She was outspoken, but nervous and wobbly at these new motions.

While Mohamed and I argued over who would cook dinner or do the dishes, Egypt argued over whether it would emerge as a democracy. We debated which kitchen cabinet would house the plates or spices, and Egypt debated the core tenets of its new Constitution. We tried to figure out how to balance whose friends to spend time with while Egypt tried to figure out how to extend the conversations within squares across the country to a post-revolution Egypt.

A quote from President Obama about the courage of the Egyptian people and the hope they inspired was plastered in the Cairo International Airport arrivals terminal. I mention this fact not to demonstrate Egyptian's feelings about him but rather to underscore the perceived support by the interim military government for the goals of the revolution. A quote like that does not get put up unless someone extremely high up approves it.

Even my most skeptical Egyptian friends, friends who did not believe Mubarak would ever step down, suddenly believed real progress would happen. Most conversations in those early months revolved around speculation about which evolving set of leaders might be the next president and might help set the tone for the future. These discussions were full of hope and were such a drastic pivot from the assumptions from only a few months earlier about the trajectory of power.

The hope and the renewed confidence after decades of economic and political oppression made the mood of the whole country feel like it was on a runner's high from a recently completed race.

However, there was also fear running like a river underneath the surface too. Sometimes in broad daylight the fear could take a backseat, but like a nagging backseat driver it would insist on barking out directions.

Recently, Mohamed and I binge-watched the series "Ramy," about a first-generation Egyptian American in his twenties who is figuring out how to balance his Egyptian heritage with his American upbringing. In one episode, he visits Egypt to get in touch with his heritage and goes to a party with his cousin who was born and raised in Cairo. He proceeds to immediately ask the young Egyptians at the party about the revolution and how cool it was to finally see Tahrir Square in person. The young Egyptians are turned off and he doesn't understand why. His cousin explains how many of the people he was talking to made incredible sacrifices during that time, some even lost friends or family members to the violence during the revolution or the aftermath ("Ramy," 2019).

When I visited the US, Mohamed and I frequently got well-meaning questions with an amount of awe, inspiration, and curiosity about "what it was like living through a revolution." We joked about it too because it helped deflect from the very real fear and panic we often felt in the months following "the revolution."

Military tanks and checkpoints strictly enforced curfews, which put a pause on the Cairo that would walk the streets or party until dawn; even time, largely viewed as a casual suggestion, was replaced with estimations of how long it would take to get home before the nightly curfew. Crime spiked. Many speculated whether the crime wave was the result of expected post-revolution agitation, the fact the police were less present, low morale given their correlation with the previous regime in the minds of many Egyptians, or some who escaped prison during those eighteen days (Kirkpatrick, 2011). Regardless, our reality suddenly included new safety considerations every time we left the house.

I played in a softball league in Ma'adi in southern Cairo, a quiet neighborhood filled with foreigners and wealthier Egyptians. The area was incredibly safe, but we were warned about walking around the area near the softball fields after a couple women were dragged down the street by men on motorcycles attempting to steal their bags.

One of my former roommates had her apartment raided by the police after a neighbor called in and said she was a spy. Several other expat friends were similarly accused by passersby of being foreign spies while walking around the streets of Cairo.

Cairo is a noisy city. Car bangs or firecrackers, noises that sound similar to gunfire, were not unusual. Mohamed, who grew up in Cairo and is accustomed to all variety of sounds, suddenly became jumpy whenever we heard a noise that could remotely sound like gunfire. He would jump up, run to the window, ask me to get down, while he made sure we were safe. It did not help that he also became hyperaware of the routine sexual harassment I continued to experience now that we were together all the time.

We wore fear like a necklace hidden under our shirts — always felt but not always visible.

Hope and fear were constant, but the feeling of uncertainty overrode both.

Activists and those that participated in the revolution expected a certain, specific kind of change. The kind of change that would lead to freer speech, elections without pre-determined outcomes, and an economy that enabled upward mobility and success. Given the swiftness of Mubarak's resignation it felt like many expected these changes to also happen quickly. Activists had worked for years to push for change while the country endured over three decades of Mubarak — there was impatience for the next step. Despite Mubarak's resignation, this was far from assured. Change, no matter how much you want it or work for it, does not happen immediately.

As much as many Egyptians detested the police given their reliance on brutal tactics, the military had a fairly positive reputation amongst the public. There are multiple reasons as to why the military sided with the protesters over Mubarak: the tilt of economic power towards an emerging business class as the economy privatized, the fairly open secret he was grooming his son Gamal to take over, the shift in power generally away from Mubarak and towards other players (Salem, 2013).

So, when the Supreme Council of the Armed Forces (SCAF) took control of the country following Mubarak's resignation, Egyptians gave them a warm reception. But the military failed to realize there was a ticking clock on how long the Egyptian public, particularly those who protested in the streets, would wait until democratic elections to replace the military with civilian rule.

Activists were stretching their legs in openly criticizing Egypt's leaders, and eventually, the SCAF became a target as Egyptians became impatient at the pace of progress. By the fall of 2011, activists began openly criticizing the slowness of calling parliamentary elections and announcing a date for a presidential election. Sporadic protests and violence became common.

Numerous Fridays we canceled plans last minute to have dinner with Mohamed's family because we were unsure we could safely drive across the city to see them, close as they were to Tahrir Square. One time we had to drive halfway around the city to get home, doubling our route, to avoid spontaneous clashes that erupted while we were eating home-cooked stuffed *hammam* (pigeon), my absolute favorite Egyptian dish; I let my mother-in-law believe I couldn't cook, or couldn't cook well, so she would send us home with containers filled with home-cooked dishes. It became normal to be driving and suddenly see a protest or clash feet away from the road without warning. One day, my friends and I shared a taxi after work to grab dinner together. The taxi turned the corner after the highway exit onto the western side of the Nile in a neighborhood called Agouza, and there were tens of people standing there holding machetes and other weapons. The seconds ticked by like hours as we crawled through traffic to clear the area. Incidents like that made a normal daily commute totally unpredictable.

Eventually, the SCAF set parliamentary elections for late November.

Despite setting a date, tensions still ran high in early November 2011 when a series of events unfolded that would (again) change everything.

On November 19, 2011, during a sit-in organized in Tahrir Square to keep pressure on the SCAF to hand over power, the Central Security Forces brutally attacked protesters. For the next six days, protesters battled Egyptian security forces on Mohamed Mahmoud Street, an offshoot from Tahrir Square that led to the feared and hated Interior Ministry. An estimated forty protesters were killed, and hundreds were injured (BBC, 2012).

I walked down Mohamed Mahmoud almost every day as a study abroad student; whenever I frequently got lost in those early days in Cairo, Mohamed Mahmoud would be a place of familiarity. Mohamed and I frequently grabbed coffee at several of the popular coffee shops on the street, a practical extension of the AUC campus. I can still visualize almost every shop in the two-block stretch away from Tahrir Square.

And now it was also the site of incredible violence and bloodshed.

Egyptian security forces claimed they were defending the Interior Ministry from attackers, but many on the ground believed the brutality shown was retribution for the revolution. The security forces used live ammunition, resulting in a suspicious number of shots in people's eyes, and so much tear gas that many protesters believed it was a stronger formulation (Ibrahim, 2012).

Like the Camel Battle, the events of that week on Mohamed Mahmoud shifted public opinion, unifying and increasing pressure on the SCAF to turn power over to a civilian government. The brutality by Central Security Forces reminded the general public of one of the primary motivators for demanding Mubarak's resignation.

Parliamentary elections were held, as planned, later that month. Cairo became overrun in the weeks leading up to the election with political banners and signs. Election paraphernalia was new to the city landscape as was the plethora of options. Given the high percentage of illiteracy in the country, each candidate had a picture associated with their name so Egyptians who could not read could identify their candidate at the ballot box. The already highly organized Muslim Brotherhood's Freedom of Justice Party won 47% of seats in the lower house, a sign of the necessary ingredient in a democracy of political organizing and grassroots support. Meanwhile the Salafi Nour Party, another Islamist party, won 24% while liberal or secular parties won 30% (Carnegie, 2015).

With parliamentary elections completed, the country turned its attention to the presidential election to take place in the spring of 2012. It felt like every conversation I had during that time with Egyptian friends centered on speculating who would win. Would Mohamed El Baradei run? Would he be able to consolidate activists support behind him? What about Khairat Shater, the Muslim Brotherhood candidate? Who among the *felool* (previous regime supporters) would dare a run? Would they even have a chance of winning? What other political parties might throw their hat in the ring now that Mubarak and the National Democratic Party were not assured to win?

In the end, thirteen candidates ran for president although only five were seen as likely contenders. Many of my liberal friends who had participated in the revolution were hoping for Hamdeen Sabahi, who led a coalition of opposition forces as a secular and anti-Islamist candidate, to pull ahead. He had to contend with the two Islamist candidates, Mohamed Morsi who ran under the Brotherhood's Freedom and Justice Party banner after Khairat Shater was disqualified for having previously served time in prison, and Abdel Moneim Abul Fotouh who had the backing of the Salafi Nour party. The potential for an Islamist winning were high following the results of the parliamentary elections, but we rationalized and hoped that would be unlikely as Morsi and Abul Fotouh would split the vote. Ahmed Shafik, the former prime minister under Mubarak, and Amr Moussa the former head of the Arab League were the two "regime" candidates, despite Moussa's attempts to side with the revolutionaries (el-Sirgany, 2014).

The speculation I heard most often from friends surmised Sabahi would pull ahead, and the Islamist and regime candidates would split votes, making it impossible for either Islamist or regime candidates to win.

The election included two rounds, with the top two candidates from the first round moving on to the final round.

The true nightmare scenario for the activists and those hoping for a secular, democratic Egypt played out: a Morsi and Shafik match-up that few expected, pitting an Islamist candidate against a "regime" candidate; it was like being asked to choose between getting food poisoning and the flu.

In the end, Mohamed Morsi won the election by a hair.

Both activists and the military, also no fan of the Brotherhood, honored the election results and agreed to support the incoming President so they could have a seat at the table as Morsi's government led the country through the process of re-writing the Egyptian Constitution.

Egypt was off to an unsteady, rocky but still airborne path upwards. Egypt passed the first test of the new Egypt —a legitimate and competitive elections along with a peaceful transfer of power. Mission accomplished. The fact that the winning candidate came from the Brotherhood, a popular but divisive organization, made for a bitter pill for those who had organized the protests. He was not the candidate many wanted or had in mind when they took to the streets around the country but the democratic process was and so he became the President of Egypt.

Egyptians' strength, courage, and sacrifice at participating in the numerous, countless, un-ending series of protests it took to get to the presidential elections, seemed to be paying off. It seemed like change was happening, and that Egypt was on a course to have greater freedom of expression and the promise of a better economic future.

Witnessing the struggle and sacrifice of Egyptians during this time made me even more protective of the rights and freedoms we have in America. I grew up watching my dad run for elected office and helping him knock on doors and phone bank. I felt proud the first time I was able to vote. These routines of democracy, the assumption of a peaceful transition of power and competitive elections, made it easy to forget the sacrifice to obtain them. Until I lived through the Egyptian revolution and the period up until the parliamentary and then presidential elections of 2011 and 2012, it felt difficult to internalize the lessons from high school history classes on the fragility of democracy.

Egypt and Egyptians taught me how much to appreciate even the most ordinary freedoms, like watching late-night comedians skewer elected leaders or casually tweeting a critical statement or knocking on doors to turn out voters or showing up to vote expecting it to count.

I prepared to finally move back to the US. in the summer of 2012, and I felt hopeful about Egypt's future, inspired by Egyptians, and educated on the importance of protecting fundamental principles of democracy.

I returned believing that the paths for both Egypt and America were clear.

They were not.

CHAPTER 15:

AN UNSETTLING RETURN

———

Moving back to the United States did not feel like coming home, at least not right away. The summer before I left Egypt, Mohamed and I packed it full of all our greatest hits. The rooftop bars in downtown Cairo, the open-air restaurant *Sequoia* bordered on two sides by the Nile, *felucca* rides, late nights at Cairo Jazz Club, hangouts accompanied by tea and *sheesha* with friends, and long walks through Khan Al Khalili and "Old Cairo" to stuff my bags with as many tokens of Egypt as I could fit in the same two suitcases I used four years earlier. Egypt had educated me on friendship, love, political unrest, feminism, standing up and fighting back, and cultural differences in spite of human similarities. Egypt was an unpredictable and sometimes cruel teacher, but she provided a master class on a range of topics.

Mohamed would remain in Cairo for at least a year so he could continue working while I started school. The only reason we were able to make the decision to become long-distance was because we had no idea how hard it would be.

Saying goodbye to him at the airport felt impossible, but at least this time I knew when I would see him next and believed he and his family were safe despite the still fluid situation in Egypt.

I moved to Charlottesville, Virginia to start a master's in business administration and would again be living with roommates that were not him. I tried to adjust back to life in America. I expected returning to America after four years to feel like a return, not a new adventure. I spent all the years of my early adulthood negotiating or arguing my way through Cairo, haggling over the price of taxi ride, crossing streets with cars whizzing by with no crosswalk in sight, struggling to communicate in Arabic, living through multiple Ramadan and Eid holidays, and making Egypt my home. I thought coming home to America would end that daily struggle to fit in and to feel like I was no longer "the foreigner."

But that was not my experience, at least not at first.

There were all the trivial things that I had missed or had changed.

Shortly after starting school, I was talking to a classmate about where to buy a miscellaneous household item since I had incorrectly thought I would not need a car while living in Charlottesville.

"Why don't you just buy it on Amazon?" my classmate had asked.

"Amazon? Don't they just sell books?" I had asked.

My classmate looked at me like I was dense.

In another moment, I was in a car with a classmate and a song came on the radio and I commented on never hearing the song before but really liking it. And my classmate looked at me in disbelief. "Call Me Maybe" had been playing on every radio station for the past several months, they said.

Smartphones first came out my senior year of college and had become big in the four years while I was gone. Smartphones were super expensive in Egypt so my first smartphone purchase was in the fall of 2012, long after many people, or at least most of my classmates, had purchased one.

During the December holidays, my youngest brother who was still in high school, asked to see my phone.

"Cat, why don't you have any apps on your phones?" he asked.

"What do you mean? What kind of apps would I need?" I replied.

He just stared at me and started downloading several apps that he felt were important for me to have. Like Facebook. Yes, I was that behind.

There were also all the little experiences that I forgot could be so easy.

Like, the grocery store. In Egypt, going to one of the big, air-conditioned grocery stores was a treat even though most of the brands and comfort foods from home were absent or expensive. Sometimes my roommates and I would splurge to purchase American pancake mix and syrup instead of the "syrup" I made boiling sugar and water together. Every so often an expat with access to the US commissary would leave the country and give away pounds of bacon, American peanut butter, or their imported liquor stash.

Walking down aisle after air-conditioned aisle with careful product placement and proliferation was like living in a never-ending candy store. Those first few months I felt like a little kid again with zero restrictions on what I could eat or buy. I bought sugary cereal, instant pudding, Fluffernutter, peanut butter, all the flavors of ice cream, amazingly processed instant meals, every variety of soft and hard cheese, and so, so much bacon.

I also discovered the meaning of high-speed Internet. My Internet at our apartment in Cairo was unreliable at best. I often would keep a webpage loading a TV show while making dinner to make sure I had given the Internet long enough to load. Reliably being able to stream videos or, as was far more important, be able to get on Skype to talk to Mohamed was like a luxury. Plus, I did not need a VPN to access American shows. I was surprised I got any schoolwork done as I learned what binging TV shows could feel like.

In America, things just, worked. In Egypt when something broke, you fixed it. And then you would fix it again. And again. And again. Until the entirety of the thing was made up of fixes. From washing machines to the visa renewal process, day to day items or processes were a patchwork of fixes upon fixes.

Not so in America where everything feels brand new because the solution to something breaking is to buy a new one, usually with next day shipping.

It also took me awhile to figure out how to connect and relate to most of my peers. There were certainly some who had had similar experiences living abroad but all I wanted to talk about was Egypt since that is all I did talk about for so long, which quickly got tiresome for those around me. I had local Egyptian, English-language news outlets bookmarked on my computer in my attempt to stay connected to Egypt (and therefore Mohamed) since the news cycle still felt volatile. Suddenly, most people I interacted with saw "the Arab Spring" as an event that had already happened and already in the past. For me and for Egypt, the aftermath of the revolution and the settling of Egypt into a new normal was ongoing. I had no one who could speak the same language even though we were all speaking English.

That first year went by fast. Mohamed visited me, I visited him. I tried, often in vain, to keep one foot still in Egypt. I still referred to Mohamed and I's apartment in Cairo as home even though we knew our longer-term plans were to stay in America. I read the Egyptian news as much as I could. The 2012 presidential election cycle in America felt oddly anti-climactic after recently living through the presidential election cycle in Egypt where the entire country held its breath about whether the process would remain transparent and fair and whether the outcome would be honored. The breath-holding in the US related to the outcome, not on whether there would be an outcome or a peaceful transition. Far less dramatic.

By the end of that first year, I made friends and learned enough about the updates in technology to not look silly all the time. I felt like I could talk about topics other than Egypt. I began to feel like the outsider I always was towards Egypt, only understanding what was happening through the news and my snippets of conversations with Mohamed we tried to grab while navigating a six-hour time difference.

I knew enough about current events in Egypt to know that President Morsi made enemies quickly. He had cleaned the house of the SCAF in the military and made a series of decisions about the security situation in the Sinai Peninsula that shared a border with Israel to make the military nervous (Hendawi, 2013). He put the activists on edge about his previously made commitments to establish a secular democracy after he largely limited their ability to contribute to the new constitution. Egyptians protested against his regime throughout the year Some of those protests ended in violence. A year in, he was not popular.

An activist group named *Tamarod* (rebel), started in the spring of 2013 with the objective of gaining signatures demanding Morsi's immediate resignation. They claimed to collect over 22 million signatures and organized massive anti-Morsi protests in late June 2013 (Meky, 2015). Morsi supporters however also came out to the streets in support of the president. Watching these scenes felt like a repeat of 2011 with little certainty of what would happen as I followed along while starting my summer internship. I caught glimpses of Egypt in between learning how to make PowerPoint slides.

The military gave Morsi an ultimatum to meet the demands of protesters by July 1st to help clear the streets of protesters. The next day, Morsi angrily rejected the ultimatum, and firmly and unequivocally reiterated his legitimacy (Kirkpatrick, Hubbard, 2013). On July 3rd, the military arrested Morsi and took him out of power, in what some called a coup, others called a revolution, and still others avoided calling it anything at all.

The military appointed an interim president until new elections could be called meanwhile Egypt was once again thrown into chaos. The next year was another bloody and chaotic year in Egypt.

Brotherhood supporters continued to protest, angry at the turn of events. A series of protests in late July through mid-August culminated in a particularly violent day on August 14th where reportedly over 800 people were killed in Cairo, mostly Brotherhood supporters. Mohamed El Baradei, the liberal leader who had been serving as an interim Vice President resigned in protest. Numerous Brotherhood senior officials were arrested, and many fled the country in the months and years that followed (Kingsley, 2014). The politics and popular opinions in Egypt surrounding the event and around Morsi's ouster were complicated and diverse. Many were conflicted. They desired democracy and a secular government, but it seemed like Egypt could not achieve both.

Defense Minister General Fattah al-Sisi, appointed by Morsi, ran for president in 2014 and won with 97% of the vote. He similarly won the 2018 election with 97% of the vote.

And that was that.

During these few bloody and uncertain months, I constantly and frantically called Mohamed to make sure he was okay.

"Where are you? Are you home? Are you safe?" I'd begin calls without even saying hello.

"I'm fine, I'm at home. I'm not going out," he'd say, a rote response after several months of constant upheaval.

If I couldn't get a hold of him, I would panic and call him dozens of times until he picked up. Usually, he was taking a nap and had turned his phone off. I felt like a nervous parent needing to always know where he was, although in fairness to myself the dangers were very real and very immediate.

His world was very small during that time, and he needed to stay close to home given the amount of uncertainty over what or where protests or other activities were happening. Some weekends, he would stay with his parents in downtown Cairo instead of at our apartment to help run errands or simply make sure his family stayed safe. Given their proximity to Tahrir Square, the area near their apartment building could sometimes have an overflow of activity.

When Mohamed came to visit Charlottesville in early fall 2013, we both again felt the relief of being together, similar to after the 2011 revolution. He finally met my business school friends who joked they were beginning to think I invented him. We joked about how we needed to stop trying to spend time apart since it seemed every time we didn't see each other Egypt had a turbulent change in leadership.

A good enough argument to me for him to stay with me.

Before we decided to get married, Mohamed and I spent many long hours discussing and debating what our life would look like. One of the bigger decision points included where we would live. Despite what many assumed, living in the US was not a foregone conclusion. His path in Egypt was secure. His graduation from AUC meant he could get a job in almost any company in the country, his network of friends and fellow alumni meant he had a high degree of social capital. He had a car, an apartment, and a job, all the ingredients for a successful life. He visited the US several times before agreeing that we would start our life together there. Ultimately, he took the risk of giving everything up in Egypt to start over with me in America because he saw the potential for us and for our future family to have access to education, quality healthcare, safety, and most importantly after 2011, government stability.

Mohamed immigrated to the U.S. He went on to get his master's and got a great job. We were living the American dream. We lived in a country where we could both say what we wanted, we could criticize our elected officials, we (once he obtained his citizenship) could vote, we could expect a peaceful and routine and even boring transfer of power from one party to another, we had economic opportunity, we could aspire to greater achievements, we could start a family, we could have health insurance, we could get a mortgage, we could drive on well-paved (for the most part) streets that had traffic lights and stop signs (even if Mohamed continues to this day to take stop signs as suggestions), we could breathe clean and mostly un-polluted air, we could trust in the water that we drank and food that we ate, and we could be an interracial and inter-religious couple free from harassment.

At least, that was how I sold Mohamed on the idea of living in America.

CHAPTER 16:

A NORMAL SANDWICH

———

I wanted to believe for a long time that prejudice remained isolated to places like my small hometown, but that was a convenient and naïve way of thinking.

There have been numerous moments I was made to feel different or treated differently because I was a woman, but I am keenly aware of the privilege whiteness provides in America and in countries around the world. In Egypt, I grumbled that the color of my skin made me a target for price gouging, but I also realized the status it immediately provided and the protection I received in moments like when I marched into an Egyptian police station to get justice.

Too often people say and do hurtful and harmful things because they mean the hurt and the harm. Too often people do not stop to recognize or question the prejudices and stereotypes they believe because no one has ever questioned them. It does not help that, typically, the burden of recognizing and responding to the hate falls on the very people being hurt.

It is exhausting and unfair.

I imagined New York, and NYU particularly, an open-minded melting pot of liberalism and progressive thought, nestled as it was in the West Village.

So, when one of my closest friends at the time routinely referred to Mohamed as a "terrorist" it took me a minute to realize the impact.

"So have you talked to your terrorist boyfriend today?" he would ask.

"What did you and your terrorist boyfriend talk about last night?"

"Are you sure you want to go back to Egypt to be with your terrorist boyfriend?"

When I eventually confronted this friend, he hid behind this being a "joke." We did not remain friends.

Shortly after Mohamed and I got engaged, I went home to visit my parents for a month to begin looking at wedding dresses and wedding venues. I expected to be forced into looking at dresses and flowers, not to answer invasive and insensitive questions about my relationship.

One of my mom's clients lectured her on my soon-to-be husband's likely intentions of simply trying to get a green card.

An acquaintance we ran into while shopping, upon hearing my husband's first name, asked whether I would need to cover my hair.

A family member grilled me on if I would be "forced" to convert to Islam or practice "his way of life."

One person asked if I thought it was "safe" to marry him.

Too many people to count assumed he was marrying me to get citizenship.

And the number of times people tried to "joke" about how many camels my parents would receive in exchange for my hand in marriage is evidence comedy isn't dead.

Sigh.

The first few times this happened I did not know how to respond. People do not typically give you a heads up before ambushing you with stereotypes and prejudice. I found that I simply needed to always be on guard, ready with a pre-defined response strategy. Thankfully, most people spared Mohamed the indignity of these questions by not asking them in front of him.

Typically, my response was to match a question with a question.

"Why would we want to live in America and not Egypt?"

"Why would I convert?"

"Why would I be forced to cover my hair?"

"Why don't you trust me to make this decision?"

Sometimes people became defensive and claimed they were looking out for me. Sometimes people bungled their words in response. Sometimes they said nothing at all and simply walked away. I don't know if any minds were changed but it was the least I could do in service of combatting biases and prejudice.

There were also the examples of people being upfront about their views about Muslims.

One vacation, Mohamed and I decided to take a trip to Alaska. We love National Parks so going to Denali National Park was a dream vacation. We spent several days hiking and exploring the park and got incredibly lucky to see the peak almost every day we were there. We traveled south to see the Kenai Fjords National Park. The bus ride from Denali to Kenai matched both parks in the breath-taking scenes framed by the bus windows like pictures.

While we are not big cruise people, we thought taking a cruise from Kenai to Vancouver would allow us to see sights and cities that are impossible to see otherwise. This is how we found ourselves sitting next to an elderly Australian couple in the dining room one evening.

We spent a lovely dinner exchanging stories about what we had seen in Alaska. They told us about all the cruises they had taken around the world. They did much of the talking.

Then, towards the end of the meal, the conversation took a hard turn.

We had never introduced ourselves formally, so they didn't know our names nor where we were from. They began talking about immigration. At that time, there had been headlines about an Australian government policy of housing a wave of Malaysian immigrants in an island off the coast of Australia instead of allowing them onto the mainland.

Without prompting, other than by the bottle of wine they had drank, they began to word vomit their opinions.

"You see, these Muslims refuse to assimilate into our culture," said the husband.

"Exactly, Australia is getting criticized for trying to keep these immigrants out but it's really to keep us safe," the wife continued.

"Yes, we have our own way of life and culture, and they won't respect that," he said. "I mean, how can you know why they are coming? Or if they are good people?"

Shortly after they began talking, I began fighting the urge to yell whatever words popped into my head, and numerous words were racing to be first out of the gate. Mohamed, knowing me well enough to know that a pile of words was hammering to be released, responded first. He is a true diplomat.

"So, tell me more about these immigrants, what is that you don't like?" he asked.

"What is it about Muslim immigrants in particular that is against Australian culture?"

"Are there other immigrants you appreciate?"

Each of his question served to get them to reveal more about their biases. He seemed at least to enjoy getting them to reveal a truly hateful set of beliefs about Muslims, although he realized I was losing the battle to contain myself.

He turned to me and said, "Well, I think it's time for us to go."

We got up from our chairs.

He turned to them and said, "I realize we have not introduced ourselves. This is my wife, Catherine. My name is Mohamed. I am from Egypt."

Despite the amount of wine they had drunk, both of them turned white. They clearly understood he was Muslim, and they had spent the past half an hour insulting both him and others of his religion.

While yelling at them would have been cathartic, Mohamed's method was highly effective.

We have spoken numerous times since about this incident. He believes arguing with people who insist on being bigoted or prejudiced towards others wastes his time and can be exhausting.

If he has the energy, he uses mock empathy to make the person feel like they have a safe space and a sympathetic listener to clearly outline their prejudice. He likes to then, and only then, confront the person with his background, often leaving them flat-footed in their response; his smile while he does this can be particularly effective.

I on the other hand have a more direct approach.

I was sitting in an airport lounge in the Toronto Airport on my way home from a work trip, frantically trying to send last-minute emails before boarding the plane. Two women were sitting immediately behind me speaking loudly enough for me to overhear. Both women were Canadian however one of them had immigrated from an Eastern European country when she was young.

Despite my best efforts to tune out the conversation, they got to a part of their conversation that became impossible to ignore.

"So, when did you immigrate to Canada?" asked the native Canadian.

"When I was a teenager," said the second woman.

"Oh, you don't even have an accent!" said the first woman.

"Thank you, I have been here for a long time," said the second woman.

"You know, we should be doing a better job of allowing people like you into the country instead of these Muslims. Whenever they come into the country they refuse to assimilate and they are ruining the culture of the country," the first woman said.

The second woman did not seem to know how to respond to this comment, which the first woman took as an opening to continue a diatribe about the dangers of immigrants from "some" countries, particularly when those countries were Muslim-majority.

My fingers froze over my laptop as my ears rubber-necked to listen to their conversation.

I did not know what to do. Do I say something? Do I just finish this email and get to my gate? What would saying something even do? I argued with myself inside my head. I felt like I couldn't just not say anything. How would this woman be aware of how ashamed she should be if no one said anything?

I packed up my bag and prepared to leave, still undecided if I would say anything.

As I was about to turn to go, without consciously making the decision, I turned to her, and in a voice that was loud enough for the people sitting near us to hear, told her what I thought of her opinions.

"Excuse me, my husband is Muslim and as are my in-laws. They contribute immensely to Canada and America. You should be ashamed of these views you so loudly are describing." I had not yet learned the value of using "I" statements.

"Oh, I'm so sorry if I offended you," she said as she did look embarrassed and seemed to fumble for the right words. Some might note, however, that she did not actually apologize for her actual opinions.

"This is not about whether I am or am not offended. You seem to be proud of being from an open-minded country like Canada and yet you yourself are close-minded," I retorted, proud of myself for making the decision to say something.

With that, I turned and walked away. The lounge was silent as I left.

I do not know if that was the right way to have reacted. I do not know if that woman felt any differently after I confronted her. I would like to believe that I shocked her into introspection and understanding.

I think the answer is likely not.

I also know how much more exhausting and hurtful these comments would be for Arfa or Mohamed. I know the unfortunate reality is often marginalized groups carry the burden for speaking up or effectuating change, and I felt compelled to say something, even if I said the absolute wrong thing, it was the least I could do.

But it was not these more blatant comments that caused routine stress, particularly since most of these comments only happened because people didn't think they were "offending" the group they were targeting. Often, the comments or actions that chipped away at feeling included or part of the group were the small little digs or transgressions, too minute to point out, and often impossible to prove.

The list of these moments Mohamed and Arfa experienced over the years is long. People assumed they didn't speak English so talked in an intentionally slow, drawn-out way. In Mohamed's business school program a guy noticeably warmed up to him after he found out he was married to me. There were assumptions they would not understand or want to participate in particular activities. Their names were mispronounced or misspelled, even when it was in their email signatures. If we earned a dollar each time someone joked about whether Mohamed lived in a pyramid or rode a camel to work, we would not have needed student loans. All these "little" examples sometimes added up to bigger question marks about being treated fairly like being considered equitably for work opportunities or promotions.

These chip away over time from feeling included.

I know one comment or witty retort will not solve anything, as much as we all wish it would.

These kinds of comments are only one part of the story though. In the year following 9/11, Muslims in America experienced a 1617% uptick in hate crimes against their community according to statistics compiled by the FBI (Alfonseca, 2021). Hate crimes against Muslims have gone up and down in the years since, with years like 2016 seeing spikes. This does not include the entire universe of intimidation. Pew Research found in 2017 that "three-quarters of Muslim American adults (75%) say there is 'a lot' of discrimination against Muslims in the US, a view shared by nearly seven-in-ten adults in the general public (69%)."

Experts, interviewed by ABC News for an article providing an overview of Islamophobia on the twentieth-year anniversary of 9/11, "link[ed] the rise in hate to the anti-Muslim rhetoric being espoused on the political stage." In the same article, one of the leading Pew Research experts also linked knowing Muslims and understanding more about the community to more positive views about Muslims.

As incidents like the 2019 Christchurch massacre in New Zealand, where over fifty people were killed at a mosque, or the killing of three Muslim university students in Chapel Hill, North Carolina in 2015 show, Islamophobia can be deadly.

This is all against a backdrop of a general rise in hate crimes over the past decade, with a peak of over 7,700 incidents in 2020 according to statistics compiled by the FBI from over 15,000 law enforcement agencies, the highest since 2008. Particular upticks in violence were seen between 2019 and 2020 in anti-Black and anti-Asian incidents.

There are, of course, ways to reduce hate and prejudice. For starters, elected leaders and people of influence could refrain from making Muslims political targets or making policies that portray Muslims as the enemies.

However, that will not be enough. These kinds of prejudices and biases need to be solved through conversation, dialogue, and relationships. I spent four years living in a Muslim-majority country. I have friends who pray five times a day, I have friends who only go to Friday prayers, and I have Muslim friends who eat pork and drink alcohol. My Muslim friends have political and religious opinions on as wide a spectrum as exists anywhere else. We eat together, travel together, talk together, and spend time together. It feels impossible to believe an entire group of people is either the same or scary when that group is humanized through relationships. This does not mean that having relationships or friendships gives anyone an "out" to still have biases, but it does make it much, much harder to have them.

When talking to Arfa about what she wanted people to know about Muslims, it was that they are just normal, boring human beings like anyone else who wakes up in the morning, brushes their teeth, gets their kids to school, struggles through the workday, makes dinner, survives a long exhausting day, and goes to sleep. She also quoted Ben Affleck, who in a heated exchange with Bill Maher in 2014 vehemently defending Muslims, said Muslims just want to "eat some sandwiches" like anyone else (Deen, 2014).

Leadership, policies, and activism certainly will help to change public opinion and reduce these hateful encounters. But human to human relationships feel like the only way to win over hearts and minds.

CHAPTER 17:

A PATH CONTINUED

I was raised Catholic by religious parents but have been skeptical of organized religion and questioning of faith ever since our local priest railed against the *Harry Potter* series during his Sunday homily. My skepticism grew once I understood what my priest meant by "pro-life" in his twice-annual sermons.

So, when I visited Jerusalem during Easter weekend as a study abroad student, I went with zero expectations or desires to have the trip be anything more than visiting another Middle Eastern city. Cairo, Amman, Beirut, and now Jerusalem was, to me, just completing a collector's edition set. As I sat in the open-air church on Easter Sunday I, for the first time, genuinely believed.

The first time I visited the Pyramids of Giza, I similarly felt moved by the ambitious achievement of human will and strength. Although I only felt that fleetingly before the horde of people trying to sell everything from a camel ride to souvenirs descended.

Despite having lived in the DC area for close to a decade, I still feel moved every time I see the Capitol building rising like a sun as I drive down North Capitol, casually glimpse the White House on my way to work or changing lanes to get to National Airport with the Pentagon filling much of the view in my windshield. Many equate DC with a swamp, a symbol of dysfunction, but perhaps I feel less bothered by the humidity of political in-fighting having grown up in humidity-prone Florida.

I don't know.

What I do know is that much of my continued awe and inspiration of these people-made government buildings and what they represent comes from living in Egypt and witnessing a revolution and its aftermath. I saw Egyptians' courage in standing up to a regime that would beat, torture, or imprison them without hesitation. I spoke with Egyptian friends who had hope for something different or something better long before Tahrir Square was anything more than a place to get stuck in traffic. I felt, along with Mohamed, the joy in believing that change was possible —real, systemic change. I experienced the fear of living in a country trying to decide which path it would go down. Either the one towards freedom and opportunity or the one towards oppression and suffering.

What I do know is I will never tire of seeing the physical representations of our democratic privilege, I will always appreciate what they represent, and I will believe in their power to inspire and do good.

And yet, this democratic privilege does not extend to all. Marginalized groups in America do not have full and equitable representation or access in our political and economic engines of power. We are not there yet.

As I watched the events of January 6th from my home in DC, memories of my time living in Egypt before and after the Egyptian revolution in 2011 flooded to the surface. Egypt herself is a constant presence; she shows up in Mohamed's almost daily conversations with his parents, in our attempts to celebrate Muslim holidays, and in the constant juxtapositions of Egyptian and American culture that lives in our household. Egypt and America live together under our roof, although thankfully Egyptian Standard Time mostly does not reign supreme (anymore).

Mohamed and I reminisce from time-to-time about places we used to go and things we used to do in Cairo, whether it was the lazy hours spent sipping tea and *sheesha* or partying until the call to prayer or drinking strawberry juice looking out at the Nile from a rooftop bar. On most days, we do not need to remember the lessons we learned during the Egyptian revolution. We don't need to revisit the relief of democracy or the lightness of freedom.

The objectives of January 6th and January 25th were not similar *at all*. But they both represent an inflection point and a crossroads.

Both days meant a country needed to choose whether to cross the road towards a democratic path or to cross and take the road towards something less than democracy, with less freedom and opportunity.

The problem is, Egyptians knew very clearly they stood at this crossroads in 2011 and then again in 2013; I worry we in the US have not fully absorbed this reality. That makes me nervous.

And I get it, when you are trying to get through the week between work, kids, friends, family, cooking, cleaning, maybe working out, and a global pandemic, leaving time to worry about the fate of democracy might be the thing that falls off the priority list. The flood of misinformation creates an alternative reality for some, while lower levels of trust in government produce greater cynicism and skepticism over the importance of caring.

The fate of democracy needs to be on the priority list right next to grocery shopping because otherwise we might not end up taking the right road. We might also get hit by a car while crossing the street because these cars and these impediments to democracy do not obey traffic rules.

What makes me so worried?

I saw the incredible courage and heroism Egyptians demonstrated protesting Tahrir Square and squares across the country on January 25th, 2011, in a country where protest was strictly forbidden and could lead to arrest or worse. Egyptians were looking for greater economic opportunity, greater freedoms, and greater control over the direction of their country. These concepts should feel familiar because they are the same reasons that send millions around the world and in the United States to the street or the ballot box every year. Witnessing my fellow Americans explicitly state their intentions of ripping up the electoral process and peaceful transition of power felt like a smack in the face to each person around the world who risks their lives and livelihood to get access to something so fundamental in American democracy. To see the continued belief and promotion in the narrative that led people to the Capitol that day feels even more concerning. A peaceful transition of power has become so routine, so normal that we have forgotten the alternative and the preciousness of its execution.

I also worry because I saw from a distance how quickly an experiment with democracy can fail. Egyptians again took to the streets in late spring of 2013 because the economy remained poor; campaign promises seemed abandoned, commitments to democracy and separation of powers seemed tenuous, and most importantly, Egyptians remained worried about what his presidency meant for their future. The protests against his presidency were a stress test on Egypt's seedling democracy, one that proved too much.

Egypt did not have centuries of free and fair elections to create the muscle memory of how to absorb the distress and displeasure of a population with its electoral decision. Despite its millennia of history, it did not have the practice of peaceful transition of power to cushion the expectations of a restless and expectant population.

So, the brief Egyptian democratic experiment ended.

In America, we have been running experiments for over 250 years. These democratic experiments happen every four years for president but happen thousands of more times for other elected offices across the country. They happen every time a newspaper runs a critical headline and every time a comedian tells a joke with an elected leader in the punchline. We conduct experiments each time we yell or post or tweet our opinions or take to the streets with clever posters. Our experiments with democracy happen so often we do not remember they are experiments and all tests of our democratic institutions and systems.

And so far, our experiments have proven successful.

We all can go out of our house, walk down the street, and stand in front of a government building and scream our criticism of an elected leader. We can vote, we can march, we can post, we can debate, we can joke, we can be right, we can be left, we can be upside down.

I worry that January 6th and the proceeding dialogue caused a crack and potentially a foundational one. Maybe January 6th and the reactions (or non-reactions) proved the experiment was and is failing.

We should never forget experiments do not always succeed or produce the same results.

My biggest takeaway from living in Egypt, a country that only briefly flirted with the idea of democracy, is that democracy is not a thing you have. It is not something that exists or does not. It is not something that is achieved or not. Democracy and all the many awesome freedoms that come with it is like an orchid, beautiful to experience but difficult to maintain with fickle challenges and requirements.

The greatest challenge is connecting this concern to our daily lives. To get people to care, to engage, and to act, means telling the story of what happens when we do not have these kinds of privileges. We are all busy and weighed down from the gaps in our system. Caring and doing something about an amorphous and ambiguous and seemingly disconnected from our daily reality like "democracy" feels impossible. Most days, the best I can do is get through the day and make sure my family and myself has the nourishment to survive. Adding nourishing democracy to the to-do list feels like too much.

Yet, I remember what it felt like to live in Egypt. I remember the cynicism about the future from my friends before the revolution, and I remember the hope and courage during those eighteen days and the months that followed, and I remember the pain of having it all taken away. I know what Mohamed and I's life could have looked like if we had stayed in Egypt and had a family. I know the kinds of options that would or would not have been available to us and to our daughter. They are not the same options we have living in America. We also know that our options are not the ones shared by all Americans.

America has a decision to make. What path will we take? Do we have a collective vision for our future? How do we get there? And do we get there together?

We are at risk of going down the wrong road. We are at risk of not bringing everyone along.

We have reason to worry, and we have reason to hope.

We have reason to feel proud and to rebuild the foundation.

We have reason to appreciate all that we have and extend those benefits more equitably.

We have numerous privileges and must protect them from assault.

We have reason to understand that some have a lot and a lot don't have some.

We are not there yet.

But, if we're careful, we can carefully cross the road toward a better future, together.

EPILOGUE

———

I watch my daughter run across the backyard, proud of herself for climbing to the top of her plastic slide by herself and zooming the short distance to the ground. She giggles, picks herself up, and then runs around to climb the slide again. I am not sure whether to stop her when she tries to go down headfirst. I am not sure she would listen to me if I tried.

I was thirty-four weeks pregnant when the world started shutting down due to COVID-19 in mid-March 2020 and when we made the seemingly devastating decision to cancel our long-planned baby shower, missing an opportunity to see our family and friends from across the country. Mohamed and I knew the right foods to stock up on and how to work together through uncertainty. We joked it was appropriate that our first child would be born during a pandemic given we got married during a revolution; our personal life events seemed to coincide with world events.

Despite our initial confidence, when we were told at thirty-six weeks that my daughter would need to come early due to a late in pregnancy complication, we desperately asked to keep her in for a couple more weeks thinking the world might go back to normal before she arrived. We made a frantic trip to the store trying to figure out what we needed to take care of a newborn. A helpful friend coached us through the basics, but still we stared at shelves that were mostly barren of the items she said we needed to purchase — diapers, wipes, formula, completely sold out.

Our careful plans for how we would spend those last few weeks before we became parents evaporated. My meticulous calendar of parenting classes and hospital visits mocked me.

My daughter came into an uncertain world filled with fear and limited hope, but we all survived. We survived being first-time parents without any kind of physical support network, figuring out everything from breastfeeding to bathing a newborn with the assistance of the Internet and video conferencing. My weekly online new moms group became my bright spot for connection and support. We survived, barely.

We marked my daughter's age first in weeks, then months, and now years. Her age similarly marks the passing of our time living with the COVID-19 pandemic. She learned how to roll over as we figured out which masks were most effective, she learned to crawl while we calculated the risks of seeing family for the holidays, and she learned to walk as we saw the first glimmer of hope with the approval of COVID-19 vaccines.

The world has been a particularly scary place since she was born, but I hope that she will not always live under such uncertainty and fear. I hope not that we go back to "normal" but that we take this moment to do better, to be better, and to create better.

One day she will grow up to know both her Egyptian and American heritage. They are different places on a map, each with its own unique culture, nuances, and differences. Both places can be beautiful and difficult, inspirational and extreme, innovative and traditional, proud and disagreeable, united and fractured, and home and foreign.

I hope she grows up in a world without (or at least with less) hate, violence, and extremism. I hope the world will accept her for everything she is and allow her the opportunity and access to pursue her passions. I hope she knows a world where her voice and her vote matter and count.

There is a vision I have not for her but for the world she will get to live in and the world she will get to contribute to and shape.

There is a path to get there.

But we are not there yet.

ACKNOWLEDGEMENTS

———

Thank you to my numerous family and friends who encouraged me to put pen to paper, who read drafts of this book in whole or in part, and who believed I could accomplish this task.

I particularly want to thank my husband Mohamed without whom I would never have found the time or space to put my thoughts to paper and who provided invaluable input, guidance, and translation verification to help ensure the accuracy of my descriptions about his country.

I also want to thank my author community who gave me early support to take this journey: Alec Manfre, Amy Trojan, Andrew Towne, Arfa, Barret Manfre, Caitlin Wampler, Catrina Vargas, Charles Morris, Charlie Goelz, Chris Fletcher, Daniel Acosta, David Besnainou, Emily Aptaker, Eric Koester, Erika Evans, Ezgi Ucaner, Farid Tadros, Fumi Tamaki, Helle, Jeanne Weinstein, Jim & Cornelia Manfre, Jonah Moos, Julia Sollenberger, Julie Reyes Harris, Kelly P. Nelson, Kevin Sanders, Leo M. Sanchez, Leora Mazumdar, Maggie Gibbings, Marisa Gerla, Michael Russell, Missy Jenkins, Myra Downing, Neal Desai, Nicholas Whaley, Noelle Herring, Olivia Anglade, Petra Mazumdar, Priya Karve, Raamin Mostaghimi, Rachelle Colas, Rich Davey, Rohan Poojara, Roseanne Stocker, Sarah Alam, Sarah Sanchez, Seung-Yen Park, Stacey Cruz

APPENDIX

CHAPTER 1

Associated Press. "Fastest-growing counties suburban, rural." *NBC News (Associated Press)*, March 16, 2006.
https://www.nbcnews.com/id/wbna11846795.

"Bunnell High Yearbook, 1968." Pinea: Flagler Historical Society, 1968.
https://flaglercountyhistoricalsociety.com/wp-content/uploads/2020/03/Annual-1968.pdf.

Cody, Pat. "Annual event Celebrates Flagler County's Agricultural Heritage." *The Daytona-Beach News Journal*, March 23, 2011.
https://www.news-journalonline.com/story/news/2011/03/23/annual-event-celebrates-flagler-countys-agricultural-heritage/64263141007/.

Hoye, Megan. "A Tale of Two High Schools." *Palm Coast Observer*, February 23, 2013.
https://www.palmcoastobserver.com/article/tale-two-high-schools#:~:text=When%20Jay%20Rodgers%20was%20in,It%20was%20the%20late%201960s.

Kent, Judy. "Links to Flager County's Colorful Past." *Flagler County Historical Society*. March 8, 2020.
https://flaglercountyhistoricalsociety.com/links-to-flagler-countys-colorful-past/.

UNITED STATES of America, Plaintiff-Appellee, v. FLAGLER COUNTY SCHOOL DISTRICT et al., Defendants, James O. Craig, Supt. of Schools, School Board of Flagler County, Defendant-Appellant. United States Court of Appeals, Fifth Circuit. March 29, 1972.
https://openjurist.org/457/f2d/1402/united-states-v-flagler-county-school-district-0#fn3.

U.S. Census Bureau. "Profiles of General Demographic Characteristics." 2000 Census of Population and Housing: Florida. Accessed June 17, 2022.
https://www2.census.gov/library/publications/2001/dec/2kh12.pdf.

U.S. Census Bureau. "Quick Facts: Florida." Accessed, June 17, 2022.
https://www.census.gov/quickfacts/fact/table/flaglercountyflorida/PST045221.

CHAPTER 3

The World Bank. "Population, total - Egypt, Arab Rep." World Bank. Accessed June 1, 2022.
https://data.worldbank.org/indicator/SP.POP.TOTL?locations=EG.

CHAPTER 4

Cook, Steven A. "*The Struggle for Egypt.*" Oxford. Oxford University Press. 2012.

Egypt Today Staff. "Experimental Unified Adhan Applied in 113 Cairo Mosques." *Egypt Today,* Febuary 28, 2019.
https://www.egypttoday.com/Article/1/66353/Experimental-unified-Adhan-applied-in-113-Cairo-mosques.

Goldberg, Ellis and Joel Beinin. "Egypt's Transition Under Nasser." *Middle East Report,* no. 107.(1982).
https://merip.org/1982/07/egypts-transition-under-nasser/.

Nelson, Soraya Sarradi. "In Cairo, An End to The Cacophony Of Calls To Prayer." *NPR,* August 5, 2010.
https://www.npr.org/templates/story/story.php?storyId=128976431.

Smith, Sylvia. "Cairo Dilemma Over Prayer Calls." *BBC,* April 25, 2005.
http://news.bbc.co.uk/1/hi/world/middle_east/4485521.stm.

CHAPTER 5

Al Aswany, Alaa. *The Yacoubian Building.* New York. Harper Perenial. 2004.

CHAPTER 6

Rasmussen, Will. "Egypt wants antiquated taxis off its roads." Reuters, August 18, 2008.
https://www.reuters.com/article/us-egypt-taxis/egypt-wants-antiquated-taxis-off-its-roads-idUSL0366203620080819.

Al Khamissi, Khaled. "Taxi." Chicago. Aflame Books. 2008.

Adham, Youssef. "The controversial street music that won't be silenced." *BBC,* June 13, 2021.
https://www.bbc.com/culture/article/20210608-the-controversial-street-music-that-wont-be-silenced.

CHAPTER 7

Central Agency for Public Mobilization and Statistics. Egypt State Information Service website. October 19, 2010.
https://www.sis.gov.eg/Story/159611/CAPMAS-Poverty-rates-in-Egypt-decline-to-29.7%25-within-year?lang=en-us#:~:text=Poverty%20rates%20in%20Egypt%20fell,Mobilization%20and%20Statistics%20(CAPMAS).

Congressional Research Service. "Egypt: Background and U.S. Relations." Updated September 30, 2021.
https://sgp.fas.org/crs/mideast/RL33003.pdf.

Fishar, Mohamed Reda. "The Wetland Book." Springer, Dordrecht. 2018.
https://doi.org/10.1007/978-94-007-4001-3_216

Griffiths, Gwyn J. "Hecataeus and Herodotus on 'A Gift of the River.'" *Journal of Near Eastern Studies*, vol. 25, no. 1, (1966) pp. 57–61.
http://www.jstor.org/stable/543141. Accessed 31 May 2022.

Hauslohner, Abigail. "Egypt's Military Expands its Control of the Country's Economy." *Washington Post,* March 16,2014.
https://www.washingtonpost.com/world/middle_east/egyptian-military-expands-its-economic-control/2014/03/16/39508b52-a554-11e3-b865-38b254d92063_story.html.

National Geographic Society. "Nile River." National Geographic Society. May 20, 2022.
https://education.nationalgeographic.org/resource/nile-river.

Tadros, Sherine. "Egypt military's economic empire." *Al Jazeera*, February 15, 2012.
https://www.aljazeera.com/features/2012/2/15/egypt-militarys-economic-empire.

U.S. Census Bureau. "ACS 5-Year Estimates Subject Table." *U.S. Census Bureau.* May 29, 2022.
https://data.census.gov/cedsci/all?q=population%20age.

World Population Review. 2019 Revision of World Population Prospects, May 29, 2022.
https://worldpopulationreview.com/countries/egypt-population.

Yaqoob, Tahira. "I Want to Get Married: Ghada Abdel Aal." *The National*, June 3, 2011.
https://www.thenationalnews.com/arts-culture/books/i-want-to-get-married-ghada-abdel-aal-1.

CHAPTER 8

Al Bawaba. "A Useful Timeline to Navigate Egypt's Sexual Harassment Minefield." January 29, 2012.
https://www.albawaba.com/editorchoice/useful-timeline-navigate-eygpts-sexual-harassment-minefield-410637

BBC. "Egyptian Sexual Harasser Jailed." *BBC*, October 21, 2008.
http://news.bbc.co.uk/2/hi/africa/7682951.stm.

Birnbaum, Michael. "In Egypt, A Backlash Against Harassment." *Washington Post*, Sept. 8, 2012.
https://www.washingtonpost.com/world/middle_east/in-egypt-a-backlash-against-harassment/2012/09/07/9292686e-f922-11e1-8b93-c4f4ab1c8d13_story.html.

Bremner, Jade. "Why Does Egypt Have A Problem With Rape?" *Vogue Middle East*, July 8, 2020.
https://en.vogue.me/culture/vogue-me-investigates-egypt-rape-epidemic/.

Egyptian Center for Women's Rights. "Clouds in Egypt's Sky." 2008.
https://egypt.unfpa.org/sites/default/files/pub-pdf/6eeeb05a-3040-42d2-9e1c-
2bd2e1ac8cac%20%281%29.pdf

Cowell, Alan. "Nawal el Saadawi, Advocate for Women in the Arab World, Dies at
89." *New York Times*, March 21, 2021.
https://www.nytimes.com/2021/03/21/obituaries/nawal-el-saadawi-dead.html.

Diab, Mohamed, dir. *Cairo 6,7,8*. 2010; Giza, Egypt. New Century Production.

Eltahaway, Mona. "Bruised but Defiant: Mona Eltahawy on Her Assault by Egyptian
Security Forces." *The Guardian*, December 23, 2011.
https://www.theguardian.com/world/2011/dec/23/mona-eltahawy-assault-egyptian-forces.

FIDH; Nazra For Feminist Studies; New Women Foundation; Uprising of Women
in the Arab World. "Keeping Women Out – Sexual violence in the public sphere."
Accessed on June 9, 2022.
http://www.fidh.org/IMG/pdf/egypt_sexual_violence_uk-webfinal.pdf.

Fraser, Christian. "Egyptian Women Learn to Fight Back." *BBC*, March 18, 2009.
http://news.bbc.co.uk/2/hi/middle_east/7936071.stm.

HarassMap authors. "Our Story." HarassMap. Accessed April 17, 2022.
https://harassmap.org/who-we-are/our-story

Levanoni, Amalia. "Shajar al-Durr: A Case of Female Sultanate in Medieval Islam".
World History Connected. Accessed on June 1, 2022.
https://worldhistoryconnected.press.uillinois.edu/7.1/levanoni.html.

Mekhennet, Souad. "Women in Egypt Face Serious Harassment Every Day." *New
York Times*, July 5, 2011.
https://www.nytimes.com/2011/07/06/world/europe/06iht-letter06.html.

Middle East Monitor. "Egypt Army Conducts Virginity Tests on Female Activists."
Middle East Monitor, January 24, 2020.
https://www.middleeastmonitor.com/20200124-egypt-army-conducts-virginity-
tests-on-female-activists/.

Muhtaseb, Ahlam. "US Media Darlings: Arab and Muslim Women Activists,
Exceptionalism and the "Rescue Narrative"." *Arab Studies Quarterly*; Volume 42,
Issue 1-2(2020).
https://www.scienceopen.com/hosted-document?doi=10.13169/
arabstudquar.42.1-2.0007.

Rachidi, Soukaina. "Huda Sharawi: A Remarkable Egyptian Feminist Pioneer."
Inside Arabia, July, 6, 2019.
https://insidearabia.com/huda-sharawi-a-remarkable-egyptian-feminist-pioneer/.

Rageh, Rawya. " Egypt Clears 'Virginity Test' Military Doctor." *Al Jazeera*, March 11, 2012.
https://www.aljazeera.com/news/2012/3/11/egypt-clears-virginity-test-military-doctor.

"Survey of Young People in Egypt." Population Council, January, 2011.
https://www.popcouncil.org/uploads/pdfs/2010PGY_SYPEFinalReport.pdf.

Tonsy, Sarah. " A Counternarrative of Sexual Violence and Harassment in Egypt:
Mobilization by and for women." *Kohl: a Journal for Body and Gender Research* Vol.
7 No. 1 (2021).
https://kohljournal.press/counternarrative-sexual-violence

U.N. Women. "Study on Ways and Methods to Eliminate Sexual Harassment in
Egypt." U.N. Women. 2013.
https://web.law.columbia.edu/sites/default/files/microsites/gender-sexuality/
un_womensexual-harassment-study-egypt-final-en.pdf.

Ali, Walaa. "Why did Nawal El-Saadawi Cause all this Controversy?" *Egypt Today*,
March 23, 2021.
https://www.egypttoday.com/Article/1/100058/Why-did-Nawal-El-Saadawi-cause-
all-this-controversy.

Walsh, Declan. "The 22-Year-Old Force Behind Egypt's Growing #MeToo
Movement." *New York Times*, October 2, 2020.
https://www.nytimes.com/2020/10/02/world/middleeast/egypt-metoo-sexual-
harassment-ashraf.html.

CHAPTER 9

Giglio, Mike. "We Are All Khaled Said: Will the Revolution Come to Egypt?" Daily
Beast. Jan. 22, 2011.
https://www.thedailybeast.com/we-are-all-khaled-said-will-the-revolution-come-to-egypt

Ismail, Salwa. The Egyptian Revolution against the Police. Social Research; Vol.
79, No. 2, Egypt in Transition (SUMMER 2012), pp. 435-462 The Johns Hopkins
University Press. 2012.
https://www.jstor.org/stable/23350072?searchText=salwa+ismail&searchUri=%2Faction%
2FdoBasicSearch%3FQuery%3Dsalwa%2Bismail%26so%3Drel&ab_segments=0%2FSYC
-6294%2Fcontrol&refreqid=fastly-default%3A8b1de3a87c95ce781bcfbd22409dd5ad&seq=8.

Ahram Online Staff. "The Face that Launched a Revolution." *Ahram Online*, June 6, 2012.
https://english.ahram.org.eg/NewsContent/1/0/43995/Egypt/0/Khaled-Said-The-
face-that-launched-a-revolution.aspx.

CHAPTER 10

al-Awadi, Hesham. "A Struggle for Legitimacy: The Muslim Brotherhood and
Mubarak, 1982–2009." Contemporary Arab Affairs, vol. 2, no. 2, 2009, pp. 214–28,
https://www.jstor.org/stable/48599577.

Dunne, Michele and Amir Hamzawy. "From Too Much Egyptian Opposition to Too
Little—and Legal Worries Besides." *Carnegie Endowment for International Peace*,
December 13, 2010.
https://carnegieendowment.org/2010/12/13/from-too-much-egyptian-opposition-to-
too-little-and-legal-worries-besides/2ynu.

"Egypt's Media Stoked Soccer Fan Anger With Algeria." *Fox Sports,*. November 22, 2009. https://www.foxsports.com/stories/soccer/egypts-media-stoked-soccer-fan-anger-with-algeria.

Elmenshawy, Mohamed. "The Future of U.S. Military Aid to Egypt." Middle East Institute: Policy Analysis, July 25, 2013. https://www.mei.edu/publications/future-us-military-aid-egypt.

Hamzawy, Amr and Nathan J. Brown "The Egyptian Muslim Brotherhood: Islamist Participation in a Closing Political Environment." *Carnegie Endowment for International Peace,* Accessed April 20. 2022. http://www.jstor.org/stable/resrep12813.

Laub, Zachary. "Egypt's Muslim Brotherhood." *Council on Foreign Relations,* August 15, 2019. https://www.cfr.org/backgrounder/egypts-muslim-brotherhood#chapter-title-0-2.

Montague, James. "Egypt versus Algeria: Inside the Storm." *CNN* November 2009. https://edition.cnn.com/2009/SPORT/football/11/20/egypt.algeria.inside.story/.

Samaan, Magdy. "Saad Ibrahim: Egypt is on the brink of revolution." *Daily News Egypt,* August 13, 2010. https://dailynewsegypt.com/2010/08/13/saad-eddin-ibrahim-egypt-is-on-the-brink-of-a-revolution/.

Shapiro, Samantha M. "Revolution, Facebook-Style." *New York Times,* January 22, 2009. https://www.nytimes.com/2009/01/25/magazine/25bloggers-t.html.

Shehata, Samer. "Opposition Politics in Egypt: A Fleeting Moment of Opportunity?" *Carnegie Endowment,* August 20, 2008. https://carnegieendowment.org/sada/21171

Slackman, Michael. "A Nation's Shaken Ego Seen in a Soccer Loss." *New York Times.* December 9, 2009. https://www.nytimes.com/2009/12/10/world/middleeast/10egypt.html.

Wolman, David. "Cairo Activists Use Facebook to Rattle Regime." *Wired,* October 20, 2008. https://www.wired.com/2008/10/ff-facebookegypt/.

CHAPTER 11

Madrigal, Alexis C. "Egyptian Activists' Action Plan: Translated." *The Atlantic,* January 27, 2011. https://www.theatlantic.com/international/archive/2011/01/egyptian-activists-action-plan-translated/70388/.

Smithey, Lee. "The Power of Nonviolent Resistance." *The Atlantic,* February 22, 2011. https://www.theatlantic.com/international/archive/2011/02/the-power-of-nonviolent-resistance/71544/.

CHAPTER 12

Committee to Protect Journalists. "Four editors sentenced to jail." *Committee to Protect Journalists*, September 13, 2007.
https://cpj.org/2007/09/four-editors-sentenced-to-jail/.

Karlekar, Karin Deutsch. "Freedom of the Press 2010." Freedom House, 2010.
https://freedomhouse.org/sites/default/files/FOTP2010—Final%20Booklet_5May.pdf.

Richtel, Matt. "Egypt Cuts Off Most Internet and Cell Service." *New York Times*,
January 28, 2011.
https://www.nytimes.com/2011/01/29/technology/internet/29cutoff.html.

Slackman, Michael. "Questions Linger in Egypt as Leader Heals." New York Times.
March 23, 2010.
https://www.nytimes.com/2010/03/24/world/middleeast/24egypt.html.

CHAPTER 13

Fathi, Yasmine. "Egypt's 'Battle of the Camel': The Day the Tide Turned." *Ahram Online*, February 2, 2012.
https://english.ahram.org.eg/News/33470.aspx.

Kortam, Hend. "The Battle of the Camel: The Final Straw for Mubarak's Regime."
Daily News Egypt, February 3, 2013.
https://dailynewsegypt.com/2013/02/03/the-battle-of-the-camel-the-final-straw-for-mubaraks-regime/.

"Obama presses Hosni Mubarak to make 'right decision' and step down." France 24.
Feb. 5, 2011.
https://www.france24.com/en/20110205-obama-presses-hosni-mubarak-leave-office.

Paget, Sharif. "Bassem Youssef: The Wild Story of 'Egypt's Jon Stewart'." *BBC*,
January 10, 2018.
https://www.bbc.com/culture/article/20180110-bassem-youssef-the-wild-story-of-egypts-jon-stewart.

"The Facebook Dilemma: Wael Ghonim." *Frontline*, May 16, 2018. Video.
https://www.pbs.org/wgbh/frontline/interview/wael-ghonim/.

CHAPTER 14

"2012 Egyptian Parliamentary Elections." Carnegie Endowment for Peace, 2015.
https://carnegieendowment.org/2015/01/22/2012-egyptian-parliamentary-elections-pub-58800.

Cherien Dabis, dir. *Ramy*. Season 1, Episode 9, "Dude, Where's My Country?" aired
Apr 19, 2019 on Hulu.

"Egypt: The legacy of Mohammed Mahmoud Street." *BBC*, November 19, 2012.
https://www.bbc.com/news/world-middle-east-20395260.

el-Sirgany, Sarah. "Egypt's 2012 Presidential Candidates: Where are they now?" *Al-Monitor.* May 9. 2014.
https://www.al-monitor.com/originals/2014/05/egypt-2012-presidential-elections-sisi-morsi-sabahi-moussa.html.

Ibrahim, Ekram. "Mohamed Mahmoud Clashes, 1 year on: 'A battle for dignity." *Ahram Online,* November 19, 2012.
https://english.ahram.org.eg/NewsContent/1/64/58444/Egypt/Politics-/Mohamed-Mahmoud-clashes,—year-on-A-battle-for-dig.aspx.

Kirkpatrick, David D. "Crime Wave in Egypt Has People Afraid, Even the Police." *New York Times,* May 12, 2011.
https://www.nytimes.com/2011/05/13/world/middleeast/13egypt.html.

Salem, Sara. "The Egyptian Military and the 2011 Revolution." *Jadaliyya,* September 6, 2013.
https://www.jadaliyya.com/Details/29474.

CHAPTER 15

Hendawi, Hamza. "Disputes Between Morsi, Military Led to Egypt Coup." *Associated Press,* July 18, 2013.
https://apnews.com/article/5b00986869134d62a19834efa21d6cfc

Kingsley, Patrick. "Egypt's Rabaa Massacre: One Year On." *The Guardian,* August 16, 2014.
https://www.theguardian.com/world/2014/aug/16/rabaa-massacre-egypt-human-rights-watch.

Kirkpatrick, David D. and Ben Hubbard. "Morsi Defies Egypt Army's Ultimatum to Bend to Protest." *New York Times,* July 2, 2013.
https://www.nytimes.com/2013/07/03/world/middleeast/egypt-protests.html?ref=world.

Meky, Shounaz. "Two Years On, Where is Egypt's Tamarod Movement Today" *Al-Arabayia News,* June 30, 2015.
https://english.alarabiya.net/perspective/analysis/2015/06/30/Two-years-on-where-is-Egypt-s-Tamarod-movement-today-.

CHAPTER 16

Alfonseca, Kiara. "20 years after 9/11, Islamophobia continues to haunt Muslims." *ABC News,* September 11, 2021.
https://abcnews.go.com/US/20-years-911-islamophobia-continues-haunt-muslims/story?id=79732049

Deen, Sarah. "Ben Affleck slams Bill Maher's Views on Islam as 'Gross' and 'Racist'." *Metro,* October 5, 2014.
https://metro.co.uk/2014/10/05/ben-affleck-slams-bill-mahers-views-on-islam-as-gross-and-racist-4893256/.

Federal Bureau of Investigation. "Crime Data Explorer." Federal Bureau of
Investigations. Accessed June 14, 2022.
https://crime-data-explorer.app.cloud.gov/pages/home.

Kishi, Katayoun. "Assaults Against Muslims in U.S. Surpass 2001 level." Pew
Research Center, November 15, 2017.
https://www.pewresearch.org/fact-tank/2017/11/15/assaults-against-muslims-in-u-s-
surpass-2001-level/.

Made in the USA
Middletown, DE
31 October 2022

13853395R00139